W9-BEY-771

MAGIC

MAGIC
HISTORY OF THE
MYSTERIOUS ART

FRANJO TERHART

This is a Parragon Publishing Book
Copyright © Parragon Books Ltd
Queen Street House
4 Queen Street
Bath BA1 1HE, UK

Original edition: ditter.projektagentur Gmbh
Project coordination and picture research:
  Irina Ditter-Hilkens
Series design: Claudio Martinez
Layout and typesetting: Burga Fillery

All rights reserved.
No part of this publication may be reproduced
or transmitted in any form or by any means,
electronic or mechanical, including photo-
copying, recording, or any information storage
and retrieval system, without permission in
writing from the copyright holders.

American edition produced by: APE Int'l.
Translation: Jennifer B. Stoffel and
  Jennifer Taylor-Gaida

ISBN: 978-1-4054-8962-1

Printed in Malaysia

CONTENTS

Varieties of Magic

Teachers of Magic

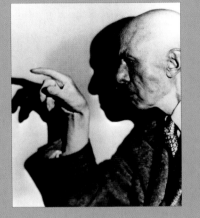

MAGIC

What is meant by magic?

The word magic stems from ancient Persian, where it meant "the art of enchantment." Magic refers to the existence of hidden forces in nature, which magicians and/or those with special knowledge, the initiated, can control and use. In human understanding, it is nevertheless part of a universal system of interdependences. As thinking and feeling beings, humans can exercise magic if they understand how to proceed. From the time of the Renaissance (fourteenth and fifteenth centuries), magicians were highly regarded members of society, ranked among the intellectuals. Magicians were educated, for they knew ancient languages and teachings, and were entrusted with the secret symbols of signs and numbers. Magicians were astrologers and knew the chemical connections in nature, so-called alchemy, and were well versed in the uses of healing and magical herbs.

Great regard and rejection of the magical arts

For all these reasons, magicians and wise women enjoyed a high level of respect and status. According to ancient and medieval understandings, the Earth was inhabited not only by humans, but also by angels and devils, spirits and demons. Therefore it was important that good magicians were able to at least banish such extrasensory forces. Magicians worked in service to kings and commanders. But during the time that followed, the division of the world into good and evil through the Church became increasingly more rigid. While all that was good, such as spirits and angels, was attributed to God, those who were devoted to magic were increasingly associated with Satan's side.

Magic is both good and evil

The Persian priests, the *magi*, predominantly concerned themselves with astrology and medicine, or healing rituals and the study of herbs. With the help of astrology, they tried to discern portents about the fates of both individuals and entire peoples. Astrologers were a kind of prophet, which was nothing dubious in antiquity. It was only later, in connection with the monotheistic religions such as Judaism, and then Christianity, that magic took on a different meaning; from then on it was associated with all "dark machinations." The increasingly dominant religious leaders subordinated the magicians as a somewhat antisocial and godless lot.

With the help of astrology, Persian magicians sought to make predictions about the fates of individuals and entire peoples. In antiquity they enjoyed high regard.

Since the Middle Ages we have distinguished between white magic and black, depending on whether good spirits or evil ones are conjured.

White and black magic, *anima mundi*

The idea of white and black magic is bound up with religious and ethical ideas. What is good? Everything white. What is black? The Devil, and evil. This distinction from medieval times was coupled with the question of whether divine spirits or demons of darkness could be invoked to support magic. Natural magic (*magia naturalis*) developed out of this distinction in the fourteenth century. Natural magic sought in every aspect of nature at first an essence of being, and later laws, a process that in many ways parallels present-day scientific study. The "essence of being," also called *anima mundi*, in medieval times referred to a universal energy that served to connect the human spirit with matter and was symbolized by a naked woman surrounded with stars. This *anima mundi* is the force that gives life to the universe. For depth psychologist C. G. Jung (1875–1961), *anima mundi* is the collective world soul in which all mythological images (dreams, fairy tales, symbols) of humanity are "preserved."

Witches' caldrons were shrouded in secrecy. In them they concocted their magical potions, and nobody knew whether for good or evil purposes. Plants, but also eyes of toads and the blood of newborns, were favored ingredients.

Microcosm / macrocosm

The ancient microcosm/macrocosm doctrine, which ultimately forms the basis of all conceptions of the effects of magic, assumes there is a correspondence between the greatest and the smallest components of the universe and humans. The famous sentence of Hermes Trismegistos is just one formulation of the idea: "As above, so below; and as below, so above." Everything that exists on a large scale also exists correspondingly on a smaller scale, and vice versa.

A comprehensive principle

According to magical understanding, a reciprocal relationship exists between the microcosm and the macrocosm. Both are composed of the same elements, whereby their material form is merely the visible expression of a hidden power that flows through both of them. Accordingly, humans are formed analogously to the cosmos. If the universe and the Earth are constructed the same way, then the stars must have a direct influence on humans, and indeed, on the course of their life, just as astrology claims.

It is similar with the individual elements: alchemy presumes that the human spirit is able to influence processes within other materials. Anyone who is able to harness this power or energy that flows through all things, great and small, is actually a magician. Those who recognize the relationships in nature that arise from similarities in external characteristics—called signs—can act as healers. The physician Paracelsus (1494–1541) believed this already in the Middle Ages,

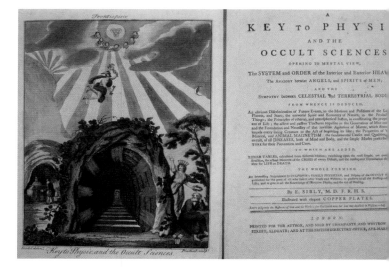

Magic books, grimoires, and secret writings have existed as long as the magic arts themselves. The ancient Egyptians already wrote their magic formulas, incantations, and spells on papyrus.

and treating like with like is one of the central ideas of homeopathy. Magical formulas are also based on this principle of analogy. The tubers of the orchid, for example, are considered to be an aphrodisiac due to their similarity to the male scrotum.

In this book

It is the application of magic, rather than simply knowledge of it, that can be dangerous. The magicians who have mastered their art warn about this. Many types of magic are presented in the following pages, including rune magic, geomancy, the Kabbalah, how to handle amulets and talismans, the use of a crystal ball and invocations (conjuring of spirits and demons). Important masters of the magic guild such as Aleister Crowley and Eliphas Levi are included, as well as the magical system of Franz Bardon, one of the last great occultists, who wrote numerous books in which exercises, rituals, and magic practices are clearly described. In addition, the significance of the famous magic circle the Order of the Golden Dawn as well as that of the modern witchcraft movement (Wicca) will be discussed in these pages. The author seeks to shed light on the rather mysterious realm of secret magical knowledge, and in doing so, to elucidate interconnections between the different areas.

Magical ritual as creative stimulation
The Italian author and Freemason Adriano Lemmi (1822–1906) had a deeply rooted hatred of Catholics. A pilfered communion wafer always lay on his desk, and he never wrote a single line before he had stabbed "the body of Christ" with his feather pen. Thereafter, his protective spirit, Sybacco, equipped with bull horns and three eyes on his forehead, appeared to Lemmi in order to provide inspiration.

Communication with angels is among magicians' areas of expertise.

Effects of magic

According to psychological explanations, magic affects us through the psyche itself: intuitions and feelings, images in dreams, ecstasy, trances and self-persuasion are the most well-known means and ways of influencing control. We charm ourselves or allow ourselves to be charmed from without. Magic is understood as something that makes us happy or anxious, and its effects are quite frequently found in everyday life.

Explanations of magical events based on the energy model presuppose a higher self, which communicates itself to us via rituals and ceremonies. Magicians interact with the universe at a level higher than the earthly one. We consider such acts incomprehensible and regard them as a kind of miracle—from spontaneous healings of serious diseases to the famous guardian angel who is said to accompany each human.

The spirit model, finally, is based on the conviction that there are superordinate forces that can carry out helpful magical services for people by means of ritual actions. A distinction is made between two forms of this model: in parapsychology, there is an animistic model as a counterpoint to spiritism. Here, spirits and other extrasensory phenomena are caused by the powers of the human soul, which are projected into seemingly supernatural occurances. The second spirit model is of a spiritual nature, which merges supposedly demonic spirits from the beyond by using magical rituals to summon them.

Anyone who is curious about yet more may ask the fairies, which are most readily found in Ireland, according to Raymond Lamont-Brown. In *A Book of Witchcraft* (1971), he describes how to bring about a meeting with fairies: "One pours a little salad oil into a glass vial; but first infuse the oil with rose water, for which the blossoms must be collected in the East. Infuse the oil with it until it is white. Then pour it into the glass and add buds of hollyhock mallow, the blossoms of marigolds, blooms of wild thyme, and buds of young hazels, whereby the thyme must be collected near the hill where the fairies are. Add the grass of a fairy throne, pour everything into the vial, and leave it untouched for three days in the sun, so that it dissolves." (1)

Like all magical formulas, this one, too, requires patience and unorthodox behavior. Fast, simple, and logical does not often bring success in magic.

Paracelsus further developed the microcosm-macrocosm doctrine, which was already known in ancient China. As everything is connected with everything else, according to these teachings, a doctor should simultaneously be an astrologer, theologian, and alchemist.

A Brief History of Magic

According to the beliefs of the ancient Egyptians, the god Thoth was the ruler of magic. Using his magic formulas, it was supposedly possible to understand the language of the animals.

ANTIQUITY AND THE MIDDLE AGES

Thoth, lord of the magical arts

In ancient Egypt, magicians were powerful and highly regarded. Their understandings of healing made their way into medical writings, and healing magic became the most common form of magic at that time (along with love charms). In an Egyptian spell papyrus, the demon god Seth is depicted as a magician holding a long staff in his left hand. In ancient Rome, the bearer of such a magic wand was called a *baculatus*, derived from *baculum*, the staff of the Roman fortunetellers. The idea that a magician needs a wand originated there. The Egyptians, however, considered the god Thoth the ruler over magic. In a papyrus dating from the twelfth dynasty (approx. 1938–1759 BC) it is written that whoever uses the first spell of Thoth will understand the language of animals. One who recites the second spell of Thoth in the realm of the dead will immediately resume their terrestrial form and return to Earth. Magic is thus powerful even beyond this life, and can also be practiced in the hereafter.

Magical pacts

Magic rituals in which one conjures the dead and restores them to their earthly form (necromancy) were still unknown to the ancient Egyptians; they emerged only in Roman times, when invoking the dead and conjuring spirits were both among the magician's competencies. The idea that one could cause servant spirits to appear does originate from this time. A papyrus from the fourth century BC describes how to summon a servant (ushebti) to make itself available and perform work for the deceased.

After the death of the magician, however, the servant takes the magician's soul with him, which is similar to different magical pacts from medieval times: the Devil, for example, wants to take Doctor Faust with him, because he was the Devil's servant for a time.

Power and influence by means of magic thus has its price, especially when magicians bind themselves to demons. This practice is called goetics. Because blasphemous rituals are used, it is a form of black magic.

Marcus Aurelius and Harnuphis
The value and status of magicians in antiquity is demonstrated by the actions of Emperor Marcus Aurelius during his campaign to the Danube in the year 172 AD. The Roman army was in a precarious situation when the Egyptian magician Harnuphis successfully cast a rain charm for the emperor, which gave his forces an advantage against the Teutons. Marcus Aurelius did not primarily give thanks to Hanuphis, but instead expressed gratitude by printing coins with the face of the god Mercury (Thoth). Magicians were thus esteemed; however, their abilities were attributed not to the person, but to their superior forces.

Especially in the Middle Ages, magicians enjoyed very high standing.
They served royal courts as advisers and fortunetellers.

The secret name of God

In Judaism, the true name of God, represented as Yahweh, is never enunciated. One usually uses the term Adonai, or Lord, instead. This is done out of reverence, in part, as God's name is sacred and not to be used thoughtlessly and thus trivialized. The other reason behind it is the ancient magical belief that the true name of something exposes the nature of its bearer. One who knows the name of a thing thereby gains power over it. This idea is found in Adam's naming of the animals in Genesis; and in the fairy tale Rumpelstiltskin, the little man can only be banished after his name is known.

In Judaism, the Kabbalah goes so far as to say that only the most intimately initiated know the true name of God, and they protect that secret, because in the beliefs of the Kabbalah the sacred name of God means absolute power over creation. Instead of the true name, the Jewish people use a variety of alternative names, each of which emphasizes a different aspect of God. These include: Adonai, Ehyeh, El, Ehyeh-Asher-Ehyeh, Shaddai, Zebaot or Tzva'ot, Elyon, and Elohim.

These names of God have also found their way into magic; they may be named, and one tries through them to effect miracles.

In the Temple of Ephesus, the magician and philosopher Apollonius of Tyana impressively proved his talent when he described his vision of Emperor Nero's murder—which took place at the same time in Rome.

MAGICAL PERSONALITIES

Simon Magus

In the New Testament (Acts of the Apostles 8:9 ff) a magician named Simon Magus is mentioned, who is thought to have had quite a large following. He lived at the time of the apostles and reputedly had visionary and telepathic abilities, as well as the ability to move objects through the power of thought. The Bible describes him as an ambitious sorcerer who wanted to be the greatest magician in the world. Legend relates that he provoked Peter to a contest, which turned out to be deadly for Simon Magus. Historic records confirm that Simon Magus founded a gnostic sect that included sexual magical practices. This may be among the reasons that the church condemned him as a dark magician and a libertine.

Apollonius of Tyana

In early Christian times, there were numerous other magicians who were also philosophers. Among the most well-known was Apollonius of Tyana, who was born in 20 AD in Tyana in Asia Minor. Many ancient authors gave him great recognition, particularly once he described to those standing in the Temple of Ephesus how, in the same instant, Emperor Nero was

Mystical flight of the soul
In the account of Baal Shem Tov, humans are created to penetrate the very essence of all life, and that is best accomplished through mystical soul flight. According to the Kabbalah and magic, the cosmos is hierarchically ordered, from this life to the hereafter up to God. The ecstatics climb ever higher in this hierarchy. According to Baal Shem, the ecstasy that allows the soul to rise from the body makes it possible to permeate all of creation, and all beings and things become visible in their interconnectedness. Humans experiencing soul flight recognize that nothing really dies, but is only transformed—death is thus only something apparent and does not really exist.

being murdered in Rome. He described the events as clearly as an eye witness. In addition, Apollonius was reportedly able to drive out evil spirits and raise people from the dead. He allegedly gave Emperor Domitian a demonstration of his great powers in Rome when he became invisible before all those present. He is thought to have ascended to heaven around 90 AD.

Albertus Magnus: an all-round magical genius

The former bishop of Regensburg was always a little suspect for the Catholic church of Regensburg; nevertheless he was canonized in 1932. Albertus Magnus (1200–1280) was born in Swabia and later eagerly studied the Jewish Kabbalah, astrology, and the magic arts. In the presence of Emperor Frederick II he is said to have spoken with the dead; he also knew how to manufacture the alchemist philosopher's stone, a substance with which one could transform base metals into gold and silver. Albertus Magnus allegedly used the philosopher's stone to influence the weather.

His greatest magical secret, however, remains the alleged creation of a speaking robot in the twelfth century. This metal device supposedly could answer questions and incensed Magnus' most famous pupil, Thomas Aquinus, so much that he destroyed it after Albertus Magnus' death.

John Dee and the language of angels

John Dee (1527–1608), court magician of the English queen Elizabeth I, concerned himself particularly with magic alphabets, especially those thought to originate before the time of the Tower of Babel. Through these, he hoped to discover something extraordinary.

In his most famous work, *Monas Hieroglyphica* (*The Hieroglyphic Monad*), the magician tries to uncover the secret of the angels who participated in creation by learning the language of the angels. For John Dee, angel magic was only a single, eternally valid symbol through which magic was raised to the level of a science, symbolically represented a triad-unity reduced to circle, line and point.

John Dee (1527–1608), magician to the court of the English queen Elizabeth I, was fascinated with the occult. His specialty was the language of the angels, described in his work *Monas Hieroglyphica*.

Baal Shem Tov: mystical soul flight and Kabbalah

The rabbi Israel Ben Elizier (1700–1760), also called Baal Shem Tov, is the founder of Hasidism, a form of Eastern European Jewish mysticism that is based on the belief that the natural and supernatural worlds stand in constant reciprocal relationship with one another. The Creator is within the world, which is only his garb. The word from the Kabbalah, the Jewish mystic tradition, "no place without him," is the starting point of the Hasidic teachings, in which God and humans have a deep relationship.

Baal Shem studied the Kabbalah, which was supposed to allow one to see and understand the basis of all things. The Kabbalah teaches, among other things, that we should find a middle way between the opposites in life and avoid the extremes. After his intensive studies, Baal Shem Tov felt compelled to go among the people doing good. On his journeys he healed numerous people, among them a critically ill boy. He attached a wax disc with the child's name to a tree in the forest. Then he set fire to it and recited a long spell. The fire is said to have burned the whole night, and the next morning, the boy was well.

Aleister Crowley is one of the most notorious wizards of modern times. Many occult researchers consider him the father of Satanism, while others see him as a mystic.

The art of magic and the magician in modern times

In more modern times, in addition to Eliphas Levi (1809–1875) and Madame Blavatski (1831–1891), Aleister Crowley (1875–1947) was one of the outstanding proponents of occultism, theosophy and magic. Many consider Crowley, who freely compared himself with "the great beast 666," the Antichrist prophesied in the Apocalypse of John (Revelation 12:1–14:5), to be the father of Satanism. Magic in the nineteenth and twentieth centuries has much to do with psychological techniques that plumb the depths of the human soul. In the opinion of occultist and magician Israel Regardie (1907–1985), a member of the magic organization Order of the Golden Dawn, the goal of magic is to become ever more deeply acquainted with one's own self and to use the hidden forces of one's own spirit as optimally as possible, thus bringing to light an internal treasure.

Consciousness raising and a better world

With our magical powers, humans rise above nature and can, according to Regardie, introduce an "ideal, utopian development of the world situation." (2) Magic to better humankind, magic to better the world—this is a basic idea of many important magicians and secret associations of modern times. The ultimate goal is oneness with God. Magic assumes that when humans set free the dormant spiritual potential within us and further develop it, evolution will take a continuously

Alchemy

Alchemy is bound up with more than two thousand years of history. According to Plutarch (45–125 AD), *Chemia* was used as a designation for Egypt; in Greek, on the other hand, it has something to do with the pouring of metal. The word *al* is an article such as "the" or "a" in Arabic. It was placed in front of *chemia* when the Arab culture adopted the art of metal conversion (transmutation). Thus the word "alchemy" has a connection to history, with contribututions from the Greek, Egyptian, and Arab cultures, before coming into contact with Western Europe in the Middle Ages. The goal of alchemy is to transform the incomplete into a state of perfection. Transmutation (the transformation of one substance into something higher) of metals and even human beings was the goal. That was true of materials such as lead, from which people wanted to make gold, and it applies to the alchemists themselves, who wanted to extend life on this Earth forever. According to alchemists, both of these—gold as well as immortality—could be achieved through "the philosopher's stone" and "the elixir of life" (*aurum potable*—drinkable gold).

positive course. There is thus true magic in expanding one's own consciousness, and that takes place as soon as we build a kind of bridge between consciousness and the deeper, hidden part of the psyche.

Visualization and alchemy

Visualization plays a particularly important role in magic; magic cannot work without it. Visualization is a psychological technique in which one "programs" the mind with mental pictures and ideas, in order to recall them later. In his book *Foundations of Practical Magic*, Israel Regardie names the ability to bring images before the spiritual eye as vividly and precisely as possible as an important prerequisite for the capacity to be a magician. In practice, people who use magic often go in very different directions with it, but they share the same goals: power and self-awareness.

Alchemists investigated the materials of the Earth, orienting themselves in accordance with the philosophies of nature considered valid at the time. They left numerous records of their studies, which affected the later development of the natural sciences.

Fulcanelli, the last European alchemist?

Alchemy is the magic of matter. It takes into account natural forces, but also those that don't have a place in well-known scientific views of the world. The alchemist Fulcanelli (ca. 1887–1932), for example, claimed that it would be easy for alchemists to build an atomic bomb, since it would only require a couple of new geometrical classifications and especially pure matter. He is also said to have extracted a completely new element from two pounds (1 kg) of iron, solely by the force of his mind and the correct substances—at least according to author Jacques Bergier (1912—1978), who was acquainted with him. Magical control of matter? Fulcanelli is said to have had that skill, and is considered the last master of his art.

The rotating galaxies have been an image of the forces of creation for all ages. Even Stone Age rock paintings show turning eddies.

Varieties of Magic

THE MULTIFACETED HUMAN BODY

The aura surrounds the body of every living creature and can be perceived by certain gifted people. Paracelsus reported this unusual phenomenon for the first time in the Middle Ages.

The aura

People with a certain gift, called clairvoyants, can perceive an aura surrounding every living thing with life energy. One of the first to write about it was the medieval physician Paracelsus. He described this energy field as a kind of fiery ball.

In the eighteenth century, the Austrian physician Franz Anton Mesmer introduced the term "animalistic magnetism," which he defined as electromagnetic energy surrounding the body. Mesmer understood there to be a direct connection between this energy and the state of a person's health.

In the twentieth century, the London physician Dr. Walter Kilner invented a viewing screen that made ultraviolet light visible. With it he discovered a weak light field surrounding the human body, and became convinced that he could draw conclusions about physical illnesses based on the characteristics of the light.

In 1939, the Russian Semyon Davidovitch Kirlian introduced a photographic procedure, which is today called Kirlian photography. It is supposed to allow research of auras of living beings, as it captures coronary rays on the exposed material.

Reading auras

Clairvoyants, who can discern other people's auras, say that it usually extends approximately 12–20 inches (30–45 cm) around the body and is oval. Strongly extroverted people have noticeably larger auras, and as people approach death it is usually weak and re-duced to a line ringing the body. When reading an aura, certain states of mind and emotions are revealed by different colors: red signifies annoyance and vitality, green stands for sympathy and prosperity, blue for spirituality and devotion, and indigo for kindness and intuitive openness.

The subtle bodies

Esoterics and those who consider themselves qualified to initiate contact with extrasensory subjects, in other words, mediums, generally speak of three subtle bodies apart from the physical body.

1. The etheric body is responsible for sustaining the physical processes. It functions as a kind of barometer of personal well-being. There are healers who are able to diagnose illnesses through analysis of the etheric body alone. When the physical body dies, the etheric body also dies.

2. The astral body processes feelings. It is formed from all the wishes, emotions, and thoughts that are contained in the human mind. This subtle body is the vehicle for astral projections or other out-of-body experiences. Upon physical death, it leaves the body and enters the astral world. It can also spontaneously leave the physical body due to accidents, comas, or the influence of drugs. The astral body is that part of us that is abroad during near-death experiences and shares the details of them later.

3. The mental body is the repository of all our thoughts, including extrasensory and intuitive perceptions. Two levels of the mental body are usually distinguished: the higher spirit nourishes itself from the universal spirit (spiritual experiences, intuition, higher truths, etc.), while the lower spirit is entirely contained within the terrestrial and material world, which is not to be taken negatively.

These three subtle bodies play an important role in many different faith traditions, both in regard to life after death and in connection with specific occult phenomena. The subtle bodies raise humans above the purely physical sphere and make it possible for us to practice magic. If human beings are more than the sum of their bodily functions, then we are also able to unleash powers that are able to exceed normal, everyday forces.

In 1939, a procedure called Kirlian photography was invented. With this process, the aura of the human body can be made visible. The image below shows the auras of fingertips and toes.

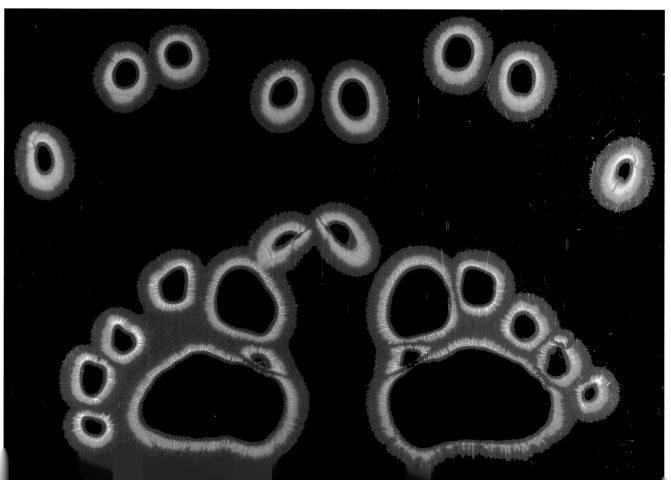

There are numerous images of witches flying on their brooms to get to the witches' sabbaths. Today we know that after taking drugs they would be able to take astral journeys, during which they allegedly met with the Devil himself.

Astral magic

The subtle bodies of humans are used for different magical acts within astral magic, which above all are intended to send the astral body on journeys and to create astral projections. According to various sources, when we dream at night, we unconsciously take part in astral travel. When this happens, the astral body steps out of the head. The astral body can then visit places in the real world without being discovered.

Allegedly there have been attempts in the USA and also in Russia to train astral travelers for the purpose of espionage. There was a great deal of speculation about this in the 1970s, but further details have not come to light.

According to most understandings of astral magic, when a person's astral body leaves their physical body, the astral body remains attached to it by a band of subtle material, referred to as a silver cord.

Astral travel

The goal of astral magic is, within an astral journey, to have an influence on other people or things solely through the strength and power of the astral body. Many magicians have reputedly been able to harm an adversary with the "punch" of his spirit, without being physically present.

Many magicians attempt to undertake astral journeys—often with the assistance of drugs or self-hypnosis. Shamans also frequently experience astral travel. They shift into a trance state which is always accompanied by loss of consciousness and occasionally even psychological damage. Near-death experiences are also categorized as astral journeys.

Similar to astral journeys are astral projections; however, the emphasis here is on overcoming space and time, for example to look into the future or the past.

Witches' sabbath: dealings with the Devil?

The word witch dates back to the Old English *wiccee*, which means a female sorceress. The theological doctrine that warlocks and witches had made a pact with the Devil originated in the thirteenth century. When making such a pact, a person had to demonstrate their subjection by kissing the Devil's foot. During the European witch trials, which took place mainly between the fifteenth and eighteenth centuries, written contracts that had supposedly been signed by both the accused and the Devil were even submitted to the "courts" as evidence. That the Devil had sex with the witches at certain places was often considered an incontestable fact: the witches gave themselves to the Devil, who took the form of a giant goat. For the witches' sabbath, they rubbed themselves with their hallucinogenic salves prepared from jimson weed, nightshade, fly agaric and mandrake. Finally, they took astral journeys and flew on their broomsticks to the mysterious Blocksberg or other mountains, where they took part in wild dances and sexual debauchery.

According to many researchers, witches date back to pre-Christian conceptions, in which Shamanism and

The old, familiar image of a witch riding on her broom isn't easy to replace. The witches' flight, however, was actually a magic journey—an effect achieved through hallucinogenic drugs.

certain cults of the dead played a role. In the Germanic concept of witches, for example, the negative traits of destructive sorcery are united with the positive aspects of healing magic.

The lines on the map represent the Earth's energy currents, on which astral travelers can move as on a highway.

THE POWER AND MYSTERY OF AMULETS AND TALISMANS

Amulets and talismans have a long history

Amulets and talismans have a very long history. They have been present in every time period and among all peoples of the Earth, and still are today. The use of

Amulets serve to protect their wearer from evil spirits, including the evil eye, as does this amulet from Israel.

amulets and talismans can be traced back to the time of the earliest high cultures. Several fantastic legends, for example, include tales of enormous giants who discovered the effects and uses of amulets and talismans even before the great Biblical Flood. According to the Roman author Diodorus of Sicily (first century BC), the first king of the Egyptians, Menas, managed to acquire this knowledge, as well. It is also written that Noah's son Cham was a specialist in the use of talismans. A modern form of the talisman is the mascot.

The distinction between amulets and talismans

Amulets and talismans play a prominent role in magic, and both are used to ensure the well-being of the person who wears them. But what is the difference between the two?

In ancient Rome, the author Pliny the Younger (62–113 AD) described an amulet as any natural or hand-crafted object that serves the purpose of shielding its bearer from accidents, worries, and dangers inflicted by evil spirits. Thus, amulets are also supposed to ward off sickness, curses, or other harmful forces. Amulets serve primarily a protective function.

A talisman, by contrast, is intended to bring good luck. Its function is to actively attract positive, favorable energies, as well as to support and foster pre-existing positive factors such as prosperity, health, or professional success. Talismans are made of ordinary materials, but an invisible and physically unverifiable energy resides in them; this power supports its owner in the desired way.

Celtic knots have no beginning and no end.

This precious amulet belonged to an Egyptian king and probably consists of three bees. This motif was already a symbol of eternal life for the Merovingians in France around 600 AD.

A short foray into the world of Celtic knots

The central meaning of Celtic knots is eternity. In addition, they are often used as magic amulets. Celtic knots have no beginning and no end, and incorporate recurring patterns that repeat endlessly—symbolic of the natural cycle of life, the world, and the entire cosmos, according to Celtic beliefs.

One Celtic knot that has become widely familiar and popular through a television series is called "charmed." The knot consists of three adjoining half-moon shapes, which hold together a ring. Three was a holy number for the Celts. The British-Celtic triskele—three intertwined serpentine lines—represents fire, water, and earth. The same meaning is attributed to the charmed knot. In addition, it is a symbol of the trinity of body, mind, and soul, which smooths the path to true elucidation for us. Another aspect of these knots is the three-fold nature of woman: virgin, mother, and wise old woman, or crone.

Almost anything can serve as an amulet; some examples are four-leaf clovers, a rabbit's foot, jewelry in the form of religious symbols, and even garlic (said to ward off vampires and evil spirits). An amulet should serve only one person, who through spiritual cleansing transfers their own personal characteristics to the object.

Talismans may also be made of a wide variety of substances, but are often crafted of neutral metals such as brass or copper and specially prepared or inscribed with words or symbols in order to serve as talismans. These materials are thought to absorb harmful or unfavorable energies and divert them away from the body. No one except the owner may come into contact with a personal talisman. During sleep, a talisman should be stored in a flaxen pouch—away from the body—so that it has some time to renew its energies.

Both talismans and amulets are important components of magic that involve people in the interaction of natural, extrasensory, and divine energies.

The ancient Tibetan mandala is the basis of Eastern visual meditation. Meditators approach the mandala from its exterior perimeter and then gradually move toward its center. As a microcosm, it depicts oneness with the macrocosm.

The origin of amulets and talismans

The word amulet probably comes originally from the Arabic language, in which cloth or parchment strips inscribed with meaningful phrases are called *hamalet* (appendages). The term talisman originates in Turkey: *talis* or *talismon* can be translated as "miracle picture." Turkish priests who concerned themselves with these objects were likewise called talismans. One can also find the word *tilisman* (magic pictures) in Arabic.

Once again, it was the Egyptians who laid the foundation for the uses and care of talismans. Together with the Chaldean, Hebrew, and Indian cultures, they were the first to depict star pictures and constellations, in addition to symbols of animals and people, on stone or metal which was to be used for magical purposes. Talismans were not only worn on the body, but also attached to houses and to everyday objects, in order to achieve a favorable relationship with gods, demons, and spirits.

Popular amulets and talismans

One basic form that is widespread is the ankh, or in Latin, the *crux ansata*. This hieroglyphic symbol means "life" or "goes." It is often shown in connection with deities, who present the ankh to the king or pharaoh as the gift of life. As a talisman, it should ensure exactly that: a long life.

Without a doubt the most widely recognized magical symbol, the pentagram is a five-pointed star found in myriad connections and contexts. It is loved, venerated, honored and—conversely—feared in equal measure by the forces of evil. It is also known as the pentacle, pentalpha, goblin's cross, witch's foot, or Devil's star. The pentagram is a universal protection symbol and the telltale mark of many secret orders.

Marsilio Ficino and his magical mandala medaillon

In the Middle Ages, the Florentine physician, astrologer, and philosopher Marsilio Ficino (1433–1499)—who rediscovered and translated the *Corpus Hermeticum* of Hermes Trismegistos—took up an old magical idea. For Ficino, the entire universe is a single living being and consists of the world soul, the world spirit, and the cosmos, or physical world. There are magical links between these three magical forces, making it possible to tap into the world spirit and use it for one's own purposes through corresponding constellations of colors, metals, and images.

In order to accomplish this, one first has to create an image of the universe. This image must include the three colors green, gold, and blue and be made of the three metals iron, gold, and silver. It is also essential to take into account astrological constellations. It must be begun when the sun enters Aries (early spring) and completed when Venus enters the sun.

On the basis of ancient magical conceptions, Marsilio Ficino recommended a mandala-shaped talisman that helps counteract the chaos in the world.

What Ficino had in mind for the object to be prepared in this way is a kind of mandala-shaped talisman (a circular symbol), to be worn as a pendant. He believed that anyone who meditated long enough on this image would positively influence the energies of the cosmos, because it counteracted the chaos that flows into the world in the form of excess, or a lack of moderation.

What would Ficino have thought of today's world, which is much more complexly structured than the medieval life he was familiar with? Although things like the sensory overload generated by modern media and computers were still unknown at that time, Ficino must have felt a similar sense of overstimulation even in his contemporary world, which by today's standards seems rather manageable.

Thus the times change, but many people nevertheless continue to trust their talismans, which help them to discern what is real and true.

Among the numerous ancient Egyptian amulets, the ankh (far right in the picture) plays the most significant role in magic. The symbols of the circle and cross developed from the ankh.

Saint George slaying the dragon, which represents evil in the world. Many hunters carried the motif of the dragon slayer with them on the hunt in the form of a talisman, in order to give them luck and success.

Representations on talismans

From antiquity into the Middle Ages, images depicting mythical events were often represented and worn as talismans in comparable situations in order to influence the course of events to one's advantage. One frequent representation was the conquest of Troy, which was supposed to help soldiers achieve similar success in battles. Hunters wore talismans bearing a picture of Saint George killing the dragon to improve their chances of success in the hunt.

Such talismans, which protect or help their wearer, fall into the category of analogous magic.

What is analogous magic?

Analogous magic is a term that refers to all magical procedures that draw on similarities (analogies) between the desired results and a ritual action to attain the wished-for effects.

This includes not only representations of events on talismans, but also numerous other enchantments. Clouds of smoke, for example, may be produced to resemble clouds, which the magician would like to form in order to bring rain to the land. Knots are tied or untied (**knot magic**), thereby strengthening or severing magical connections. In **sympathetic magic**, dolls are used to represent specific people with whom a person has a close relationship. The dolls are made including something from this person, such as hair, nail clippings, or articles of clothing. Anything done to these dolls should have corresponding effects on the living people, either to help or to harm them. One notorious example is sticking pins into a **voodoo doll**, which is thought to cause immediate pain to the person the doll represents, though voodoo is more often used in positive ways.

Even folk dances were frequently suffused with analogous magic. High jumping by the dancers was connected with the tall growth of plants, and thus a rich harvest, to name just one example.

With the help of voodoo dolls, most of which represent a specific person, sharp needles and magical words can be used to torment the dolls until that person submits to one's will.

The famous eye of the god Horus is another symbol that is considered sure protection against the "evil eye." At the same time, it preserves one's own health. Even today, this symbol is often worn in the form of various pieces of jewelry.

THE EVIL EYE

A special sort of curse

Curses are the purposeful attempt to arouse demons in order to punish one or more people with their assistance. The effect of a curse is frequently psychological in nature, and there are many diverse forms of curses, one of which is the "evil eye."

Many curses require the use of certain articles in order to be effective, often in combination with ritual actions. In ancient times, wishes and curses were usually inscribed on special tablets, and then secretly placed in the proximity of the intended recipient. The Jewish prophet Jeremiah, for example, wrote down all the disastrous things that would happen to Babylon on a sheet of parchment. Then he charged his servant, Seraia, with the mission to bring it to Babylon, read the text aloud, tie the page to a stone, and throw it into the Euphrates River. Babylon would then sink just like the stone, never to rise again. The Teutons used square plates of bone with runic inscriptions for similar curses.

Most curses, however, are spoken aloud. Centuries ago in Ireland, there were even certain women who would pronounce curses on behalf of a third party. One paid a princely sum for these services, and the recipients of the curse were more often shocked than amused.

But curses through the evil eye belong in a category of their own, for they are neither spoken nor require rituals to take effect; a look alone casts the spell. Nonetheless, it is a widespread form of black magic, and its mysterious force can affect not only humans, but also animals and plants.

The power of the eyes

Because the eyes are thought to have the ability to reveal hidden inner forces, they are generally understood to have special power.

The dreaded evil eye plays a role in the mythologies of numerous ancient civilizations: in ancient Scythian and Illyrian texts one finds descriptions of women whose angry gazes could kill. Ancient Iranian mythology contains the she-demon Agash, who personifies the evil eye, and among the Celts the one-eyed giant Balor was considered someone who could use his eyes as a deadly weapon. Medusa is a well-known figure in Greek mythology—all who caught sight of Medusa were turned to stone. The legendary basilisk, a fearsome serpent said to have hatched from a shell-less rooster's egg tended by a toad, also possessed a deadly gaze. The basilisk is regarded as something of an exception, because the ability to kill through the gaze alone is seldom found among animals. This is a predominantly human capacity, often attributed to those who are already suspected of practicing witchcraft, and more frequently older women than older men.

Some people are thought to have such an intense evil eye that they endanger others merely by looking at them, often without intending or even being aware of it. The evil eye doesn't always kill; it can also cause illness or wasting away.

Preventive measures

Pearls, red bands, and coral necklaces promise protection against the harmful magic of the evil eye.

In the Middle Ages, witches who were suspected of the evil eye were fought by cutting open their forehead with a knife.

In the Mediterranean region, people counteract the evil eye with a certain hand gesture, in which the index finger and the little finger are outstretched. This defense is said to be very helpful.

Interacting with spirits and demons was always an important part of primitive magic. They were summoned in ritual dances, in which the dancers wore eerily beautiful masks. The magicians often danced in a deep trance state.

MAGICAL RITUALS AND SYMBOLS

Content and meaning

The mysteries of many modern secret societies, such as those of the Freemasons or Druid orders, is an esoteric knowledge that is to a large extend encoded in symbols and rituals. Those who believe in their power assume that the symbols communicate a certain reality, which can only be fully expressed through vehicles such as fairy tales, myths, Gnostic parables, symbols, images, rituals, or dream appearances. The assumption that symbols and rituals possess a deep measure of truth is at the very core of all esoteric secret societies. According to them, the truth is not found in fixed stances, but instead in the search itself. This ongoing search is frequently expressed by the Freemasons and other secret societies through repetitive wanderings, so-called mystical journeys.

Taking magical symbols seriously

The symbol, which can be contained in a sentence, a word, or in a gesture, is very similar to a ritual. Articles of clothing, certain colors, places, and various objects are all carriers of meaning; these meanings differ according to different secret societies. That means that these symbols are only effective within each respective system, so that the interpretation of a triangle or a symbolic sun is not identical for a Freemason, a Rosicrucian, and a modern witch. The effects and power of symbols are taken absolutely seriously—otherwise they would not be effective. Understood in this way, symbols and rituals draw upon the entire human being, and mean more than simply understanding the "rules of play."

The all-seeing eye that forms the point of a pyramid is printed on the one dollar bill. The symbol originally comes from the German *Illuminati* and was adopted by the Freemasons, some of whom were among the founding fathers of the USA.

The knowledge that symbols and rituals contain hidden truths is a part of all secret societies. They assume that symbols significantly expand reality, including the skull on the gravestone pictured here.

The ancient Egyptian god Osiris has been invoked by numerous magicians. Aleister Crowley claimed to be able to unite with Osiris through a specific ritual.

The magic of ritual

The ritual is a sacred process which can only be fully understood by those who inwardly comprehend it. A ritual thus cannot be divulged to the ignorant, or, to express it another way: no magic is done by simply going through the motions. Ritual is always taken seriously and solemnly. The power of its magic lies in its more or less frequent repetition of a formulaic sequence of events.

Magical beings like this siren are found in many churches in Western Europe. For people in medieval times, nature was populated with all kinds of supernatural beings, such as elves, gnomes, and goblins.

A magical ritual frequently consists of a long text or poem, followed by calling on the elementary spirits who reside in the four elements of air, fire, earth, and water (invocations) and an elaborate conclusion (peroration). Like the bornless ritual described below, these invocations of the elementary spirits, also called elementals (sylphs, salamanders, gnomes, and undines respectively) can last 70 to 80 minutes.

The bornless ritual

The conclusion of the bornless ritual, which was a favorite of Aleister Crowley's, consists of a great invocation or peroration: "I am He, the Bornless Spirit, having Sight in the feet: strong, and the immortal Fire! I am He, the Truth! I am He, who hates that evil should be wrought in the world! I am He, that lighteneth and thundereth. I am He, from whom is the shower of the life of Earth. I am He, whose mouth ever flameth. I am He, the begetter and manifester unto the Light: I am He, the grace of the World: the heart girt with a serpent is my name!" (3)

The dangerous Tibetan practice of chod encourages Buddhist seekers to separate radically from false attachment to the self, especially the physical body. That takes place by beckoning all evil spirits and urging them to eat one's own body.

This ritual conjures the ancient Egyptian god Osiris, who unites with the magician, conferring power on him or her. It is as if the light of the god is tranferred to them. Behind this is the idea that through rituals, the magician can unite with all of life in space and time. Ecstasy and illumination, spiritual enlightenment, are the true goal.

The dangerous practice of chod

The danger inherent in some rituals described in magical literature is demonstrated by the Tibetan practice of chod, which was practiced by Alexandra David-Neels (1868–1969), and intrepid researcher occupied with occultism during the fourteen years she lived in Tibet.

By means of chod, the seeker should be severed from all false conceptions of the ego for all time—and that is meant as radically as it sounds: *chod* means "cutting through." In this ritual, one calls all evil spirits and invites them to eat one's body. The chod rite is practiced in deep meditation, in which the body is understood to be fat and ugly, the hook from which all one's vices are hung. Then one visualizes a certain goddess of wisdom, who cleaves the head from the body and hacks the remainder into pieces. Everything is thrown into one's own cranium, which is placed over a fire, like a pot. The unimaginable astral light that emanates from the offering attracts a wide array of various spirits. (In spiritism, spirits are always attracted by a light that streams from the soul.)

The chod ritual requires great self-discipline and a strong character. It is often practiced in cemeteries or other unsettling locations, and is regarded as a dangerous magical practice, which, if practiced incorrectly, can lead to psychological disturbances.

MAGIC PRACTICES
OF THE TEUTONS

The magic of right and left

The Teutonic people are distinguished by a whole series of magical practices: charms, rune magic, fertility charms, soothsaying, magic for defamation, healing, causing harm, and death.

Weather and rain spells certainly count among the oldest magical dealings. A collection of medieval texts in which the old Teutonic magical rituals are recorded reveals more: "Did you do what certain women tend to do? When they need rain and have none, they assemble young girls and choose a small virgin as the leader. They expose her and lead the naked one outside the village to a place where hyoscamus (henbane) can be found. Using the small finger of the right hand, they uproot the herb and fasten it to the small toe of the right foot with some kind of band… finally they lead

the appointed virgin, naked, as she is, and using her feet like those of a crab returns from the river back to the village on her hands." (4)

It is noticeable that left and right are assigned special importance. For the Celts and the Teutons, the right side was the side of light and life, while the left was associated with the shadow side, or death. This is why the Teutonic girl could use only her right hand to pick the herb, so that the force of light could have an effect. Consuming henbane produces acoustic hallucinations that are very similar to the sound of rain. Walking like a crab means traveling backwards, which prevents the magic from turning itself around and thus becoming ineffective. The magical effect of these rituals unfolds by programming the desired outcome in the same way—through a ritual which is eternally the same.

Stone Age mounded graves—called *tumuli*—served as entrances to the realm of the dead, but also provided access to supernatural beings such as elves, for example. Such places were preferred spots for practicing magical rituals.

Death magic

The extraordinary importance of executing magical practices accurately is clearly seen in texts describing death magic. Such records describe, for example, women who attempted to kill their husbands or their enemies by grinding wheat backwards in the mill, in the direction counter the course of the sun. Then they baked bread from this flour, which the men ate. Turning a mill to the left was though to eventually bring about death, because the forces of life are made weaker and become shadowy on the left side. The left side is the evil one, the aspect that inhibits the course of life. As soon as something is consciously made or done on the right side, it serves to strengthen— whether it is love, life, or health.

Interestingly, there are certain parallels to this phenomenon in current brain research: language skills are apparently strengthened when we turn our heads to the right, which increases blood flow to the left side of the brain. Conversely, spatial skills are accentuated by turning the head to the left (which activates the right hemisphere).

Odin rides on his eight-legged horse Sleipnir. The Teutonic god manifest himself in different forms: as the god of poetry, god of death, god of war, and the god of magic, runes, and ecstasy.

Fertility and love charms

Fertility and love charms have been of tremendous importance in every time period. Teutonic fertility spells involved burying fertilized eggs in the earth so that their fertility would be transferred to the meager soil. They would also strike fields, trees, animals, and even people with a fresh rod so that the driving force of the shoot would be transferred to them. The basic idea behind love charms was that blood, as a substance of the soul or vehicle of life, was an important part of every form of magic. Anyone who mixes their blood with that of another person is magically bound to them. For this reason, many a Teutonic woman mixed her menstrual blood with the food or drink of a man, in order to kindle or increase his love for her.

Feng shui is the Asian form of Western geomancy. Before a house is built, it is important to clarify whether the earth spirits find the proposed site favorable.

GEOMANCY – THE ART OF DIVINATION BY EARTH

A new old art

Originally, the term geomancy indicated foretelling the future by means of sounds from the interior of the Earth, such as those made by earthquakes. Geomancy is the Western equivalent of the Eastern art of feng shui, although it has been almost entirely forgotten for the past 200 years, at least in Europe.

Contemporary esoterics have brought geomancy back into our awareness. Now, however, the term indicates knowledge of the lines and places of power on Earth, which itself is understood to be a living organism, the mother Gaia. These currents of power are called ley lines, and some people believe that they traverse the Earth much like nerve pathways.

Our ancestors, such as the Celtic Druids, probably had similar conceptions; to that extent, geomancy re-

mains the term for an old science that helped people in earlier times and cultures successfully live in harmony with nature and its invisible forces.

Dowsing rods and Earth rays

An important precondition for the idea of being in tune with nature is the ability to discern the qualities of a particular place and to recognize the laws of nature. One of the tools that makes this possible is the dowsing rod, among other things. People have also discovered that a great number of old churches and cult sites, menhirs (megaliths), and prehistoric graves are geographically situated along a series of straight lines. Experienced geomancers can make connections between these lines and the vegetation that grows nearby: fir and spruce trees try to avoid the Earth's rays, which are thought to result from waterways and ore veins that cross each other underground, while elders, stinging nettle, and hazelnut seek them out. The Earth's energy is generally regarded as harmful.

What purpose does geomancy serve?

In the opinion of contemporary geomancers and dowsers, the connection of all human beings with nature and the transcendent worlds, which was originally so obvious as to be taken for granted, has been increasingly obliterated in the course of the development of Christianity. Eventually, the knowledge of geomancy was only accessible to a few inaugurates, who used, guarded, and preserved this wisdom. With the help of newly rediscovered geomancy, which can be translated as "feeling for the Earth," it is once again possible to live and work in harmony with the existing patterns and rhythms of the Earth and nature, furthering the well-being of all involved. In Japan, feng shui

is regarded as a science and no builder ignores it. The modern feeling of separation from nature can be overcome by experiencing the reciprocity between people, the Earth and the cosmos, and by fully comprehending how alive and divine the Earth is.

Geomancy and Earth healing

The goal of contemporary geomancy is to heal. A well-known keyword is "Earth healing," in which architecture, among other things, plays an important role, as it forms our immediate environment. Insightful design respects the subtle forces that inform a place, either maintaining or re-establishing them.

In addition, the proper arrangment of colors and shapes, mass and proportions, symbols and materials can strengthen the connections to heaven and Earth, adjust imbalances, and simply create more vital and harmonic spaces. To accomplish this, one can invite an experienced geomancer or feng shui practitioner to restyle one's home, office, or garden in accordance with these principles.

The modern feeling of separation from nature is overcome by feng shui. A special compass helps practitioners discern to what extent unfavorable interactions between people, the Earth and the cosmos can be circumnavigated.

THE CHINESE I CHING

History and origin

The I Ching, also known as the *Book of Change* or *Book of Transformations*, is the oldest surviving writing about philosophy, cosmology and prophecy in China. The origins of the work go back as far as the turn of the second to the first millennium BC, but fascination with this book of wisdom has remained strong even into modern times. In the book *The Inner Structure of the I Ching*, by Lama Anagarika Govinda, it is written that, "the most incredible characteristic of the *Book of Changes* is that it does not seek what is immutable and eternal, but instead establishes change itself as the basic principle of the universe." (5) The Chinese took the bull by the horns, so to speak, and discovered the eternal in the principle of change. Nothing remains as it is, and that is as it should be. "Everything flows," the Greek philosopher Heraclitus already remarked. "We are all mortal, as long as we fear death; but in the moment we submit to the eternal rhythm of the universe in which we live, we are immortal," Govinda writes. (5)

The secret of the I Ching

The basis of the I Ching is the polarity and contrast of the two principles yin (female) and yang (male). Everything that is and everything that happens develops from the interaction of these two main principles of the cosmos. Human nature can also be explained by the interaction of yin and yang. In the *Book of Changes*, yin is represented by a broken line, and yang by a continuous line. When these two principles are combined in multiples of three to form written Chinese characters, there are eight basic possibilities (yin-yin-yang, yang-yin-yang, etc.), which are called the eight trigrams of the I Ching.

Asian religions discovered the eternal in change, because nothing in the world remains as it is. They rely on the *Book of Changes*, or I Ching, which is considered the oldest philosophical writing in China.

The trigrams of the I Ching

Number	Name	Function	Image	Nature	Figure
1	Sun	Perception	Wind/Grass	Gentle	
2	Li	Thought	Wood/Fire	Attaching	
3	Tui	Feeling	Lake	Serene	
4	K'un	Will	Earth/Cave	Yielding	
5	Ken	Body	Mountain	Being still	
6	K'an	Soul	River/Water	Depths, abyss	
7	Chen	Spirit	Thunder/Lightning	Exciting	
8	Chien	Awareness	Heaven	Creative	

Practice of the I Ching

The *Book of Changes* is a collection of oracle texts which only make sense when they are read in relation to a certain question. Therefore, a person should only consult the oracle if they are actually wrestling with unresolved questions. The I Ching is queried either by casting fifty stalks of yarrow eighteen times altogether, or by tossing three identical copper coins six times. In this case, the value of each toss is noted—heads has the value three, tails is two—and from the results a hexagram is constructed from top to bottom. When all throws have been completed, one asks the oracle for an answer to their question, and then reads the words of the I Ching that correspond to the hexagram that has taken form.

The universal life force consists of the two basic principles of yin and yang. Yin is the feminine principle and yang the masculine. Balanced interplay of both forces leads to harmony.

The Kabbalah, originally a form of Jewish mysticism, is experiencing increased popularity in the West, which is illustrated by the amount of literature on this theme.

THE KABBALAH

Origin and meaning

The word *Kabbalah* is derived from an older one meaning "receive, take" and means "tradition." This is in contrast to the Torah, the first five books of the Bible and the first of the three parts of the Hebrew Bible, which contains God's direct instructions to the Jewish people (the others are the Prophets and the Writings). Kabbalah, on the other hand, is an esoteric and speculative branch of Jewish mysticism.

While the subject of the Torah, the written religious and legal doctrine, is the will of God, which a pious Jew must obey, Kabbalah stives to understand God's very being. That sounds abstract, but the Kabbalah claims to hold the key to hidden wisdom, knowledge of all spiritual teachings that decodes all secrets of the universe and answers all the basic human questions.

The nature of the Kabbalah

The basic teachings of the Kabbalah try to grasp the secret nature of God and discern the cosmological structure of the world. Kabbalists understand God as the force of all of reality, while the Spanish Kabbalists who followed Moses de León regarded the Devil as their powerful opponent. People are free to decide which side they will adhere to.

The Kabbalah offers its initiates the opportunity to recognize links between humans and the universe, between creature and creator. These links are understood as forces or spirits, with whose assistance the created world can also be shaped by human beings; but only if the people are capable of subservience. For this, certain powers such as angels, genies, or demons must be invoked.

The Zohar

The fundamental text of the Kabbalah is the *Zohar* ("illumination"), a mystical text that was recorded in the thirteenth century. It was most likely written by the Spanish mystic Moses de León, or Moshe ben Shem Tov (1250–1305), and supplies a summary of all well-known Kabbalic teachings at that time. Written in Aramaic, the language Jesus spoke, the book consists of 2,400 densely recorded pages. It concerns, among other things, the hierarchy of evil, the "unholy sephiroth," which are in stark contrast to the ten divine sephiroth, the emanations (or enumerations) of God, ten attributes that originate in the immutable Divine One and bring luck and benediction to humans. These ten levels are the primary subject of the Kabbalah.

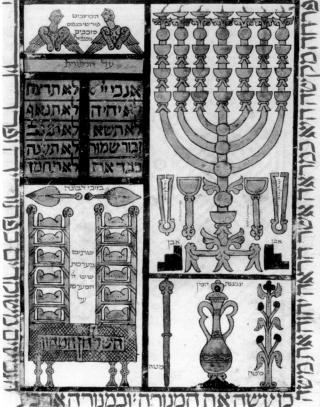

Jewish ritual objects, such as the menorah, a seven-armed candlestick, which the Romans brought to Rome following their destruction of the Temple of Jerusalem in the year 70 AD, and which has been missing since that time.

The pentagram ritual (see the discussion of Aleister Crowley and the Order of the Golden Dawn on pages 66 and 85) is one such invocation. In it, demons are aroused through magical incantations (evocations) in order to make themselves of service.

According to the *Zohar*, the most important of the Kabbalistic texts, all powers of the universe are awakened or reawakened through names and symbols. In the Kabbalah there are twenty-two powers of creation (the letters of the alphabet). In both written and spoken form, these contain the energies of the universe and allow us to make use of them.

The Kabbalah promises hidden wisdom, a treasury of knowledge of all spiritual teachings, which decodes all secrets of the universe and answers the fundamental questions that plague humanity.

The Torah is the holy book of God, which may not be touched with bare hands. Convinced that God speaks Hebrew, the Kabbalist makes use of the magical power that is inherent in each and every letter in this most holy of texts.

Gematria, or practical Kabbalah

There is a lovely anecdote about sephiroth that demonstrates the possibilities of gematria, the application of Kabbalistic knowledge. It is important to understand that in gematria, each Hebrew letter possesses a specific numerical value. This makes it possible to exchange words with the same numerical value (the sum that results from adding the numerical value of each individual letter), thus allowing us to understand the secret sense of a passage.

Naturally, this system can also be transferred to other alphabets or languages, but Kabbalists are convinced of the fact that God speaks Hebrew.

The first letter of the Hebrew alphabet is aleph. Each letter in this alphabet is an instrument of power. Indeed, the Hebrew word for letter means something like "vibration" or "pulse."

The interpretation of "amen" as an example of Kabbalic process

For Kabbalists, God is the "One," because he is the origin and beginning of all that is. "One" is *achad* in Hebrew. The word is spelled as follows: aleph (1) + cheth (8) + daleth (4). The sum of the numerical value of the three letters is the number 13. The word *ahavah* means "love" and is spelled aleph (1) + heh (5) + beth (2) + heh (5). The numerical value of the letters is also 13. From this, Kabbalists conclude that love and unity have the same nature. Further still: if one adds these numbers, one obtains 26, the numerical value of YAHWE = God.

The anecdote about sephiroth mentioned at the beginning concerns the Latin word *amen*. The origin

The topic of the Yetzira, a short book, is the creation of the world and humankind. Those who attain this knowledge can, according to Kabbalists, attain the source of all being, God himself.

The ten "levels" of God

One of the most important basic concepts of the Kabbalah is the sephiroth, which denote the ten attributes of the mysterious God, the absolute, the highest one, called *Ein-soph*, literally "without end." The ten sephirot are understood as forming a tree, the Tree of Life. Each one represents an aspect of divine being, through which the hidden world of the absolute one, i.e. God, is revealed. The individual stages (sephirah) of the Kabbalic tree, in order, are:

Kether	=	Crown of divinity
Chokmah	=	Wisdom, or original idea of God
Binah	=	Intelligence or understanding
Chesed	=	Love or mercy of God
Din	=	Power or strength of God
Tiphereth or Rakhamim	=	Beauty
Nezach	=	Endurance or triumph of God
Hod	=	Majesty or glory of God
Yesod	=	Foundation of all God's active and creative powers
Malkuth	=	the Kingdom of God

These ten sephiroth constitute the mystical Tree of Life. The qualities of the sephiroth also exist in individual people. The different parts of the human body are manifestations of an inner, spiritual being, which is symbolically represented by Adam Kadmon, the primordial human.

and meaning of this word, which is uttered by both Jews and Christians, is unexplained. It is commonly translated as "so be it!" For Kabbalists, however, "amen" is always a plea, a request of God. The Hebrew letters of this word read aleph, mem, and nun; these same three are the initial letters of three Hebrew words that are associated with God. The translation of the Kabbalists would therefore be "Lord, faithful king!"— in other words, the Kabbalic sense of "amen." Its numerical value is 91, and the sum of its digits is 10. That once again refers to the ten sephiroth, and thus to God.

NUMEROLOGY AND EXORCISM OF DEMONS

Numerology and Kabbalah

Numerology, a theory of the mystical importance of numbers, is originally founded on the Hebrew alphabet, in which each letter has a numerical value. The Greek poet Terentianus Maurus (around 200 AD) used numerology to "prove" that his worst enemy, Thamagoras, was even worse than the plague (Greek *loimos*), because Thamagoras had the numerical value of 425, and *loimos* only 420. This is one way to make use of number magic!

Demonology and the Lesser Key of Solomon

In the traditional Christian conception, demons are "sons of God," fallen angels who mingled with the daughters of humans and were cast out by God. In

Numerology in everyday life

Modern numerology is not only concerned with the numerical values of names, but also a form of divination that tries to foretell a person's character and life path using their birthdate. The occultist Louis Hamon, known as Cheiro (1866–1936), for example, followed such a path, and was at the same time a master of the art of hand reading. The date of birth is the key number, whereby this fate can only be accepted, but not changed. The number corresponding to a person's name, on the other hand, characterizes one's spiritual nature. Life rhythms can be forecast according to numerology by adding the numbers of the birth year. For someone born in 1958 (1+9+5+8=23), according to numerology, the year 1981 (1958+23) will be very significant, as well as 2004, 2027, etc.

addition, these angels abetted the Devil, who thus became the leader of a great, dark realm. The New Testament records that Jesus drove out numerous demons that had taken possession of humans, for example in the Gospel of Luke: "Now he was casting out a demon that was dumb; when the demon had gone out, the dumb man spoke, and the people marveled." (Luke 11:14)

In Jewish faith, these demons remain a presence. Wednesdays and Sabbath nights are considered to be particularly dangerous, since 18,000 demons are out and about at these times.

An important source for protection from and banishment of demons is the *Lesser Key of Solomon*, a book also well known as the *Lemegeton*. Israelites brought this old magic text, or grimoire, from Egypt. Among members of the Golden Dawn, the introductory

In numerology, also called arithromancy, numbers are the key to our being and to the course of our lives.

Hollywood has also dealt with the theme of exorcism: the film
The Exorcist is based on real events.

chant is practiced as an individual rite called the bornless ritual (the ritual of the unborn; see also page 32).
In this case, however, the opposite goal is desired: the
demons are invoked, rather than expelled.

An age-old exorcism of demons

Before performing an exorcism of demons, the names
of the individual demons are written on a sheet of
paper, which is stretched across the forehead from
temple to temple. Facing northward, the individual
names are called, and the ritual words are spoken
loudly and clearly: "Hear me, and make all spirits
subject unto me: so that every spirit of the firmament
and of the ether, upon the Earth and under the Earth,
on dry land and in the water, of whirling air, and of
rushing fire, and every spell and scourge of God may
be obedient unto me.

Thee I invoke, Akephalos [Greek; refers to the bornless one], thee that created the Earth and Heavens, the
night and the day, the darkness and the light.

Thou art OSORRONOPHRIS, whom no man has seen at
any time.

Thou hast distinguished between the just and the
unjust. Thou hast made female and male. Thou hast
produced the seed and the fruit. Thou hast formed
men to love one another, and to hate one another.

I am MOSHEH your prophet, unto whom thou didst
commit thy mysteries, which ISHRAEL fulfills. Thou hast
produced the moist and the dry, and that which
nourishes all created Life. Hear thou me, for I am the
angel of PAPHRO OSORRONOPHRIS; this is thy true name,
handed down to the prophets of ISHRAEL. Hear me:

AR, THIAO: RHEIBET: ATHELEBERSETH:

A: BLATHA: ABEU, EBEU: PHI:

CHITASOE: IB: THIAO

Hear me and turn this spirit away. I invoke thee, ter-
rible and invisible God, who dwellest in the void…"(6)

The text is substantially longer in the original,
names many additional ancient gods, and—recited in
a ritual context—conveys an archaic atmosphere. Although it is an exorcism, it is nevertheless a highly
impressive ancient spell.

A crystal ball is used for gazing into the past and future, and has long been a valuable tool for fortunetellers.

THE CRYSTAL BALL

A guide for gazing into the past and future

For centuries, even millenia, the crystal ball has been used by purported witches as well as wise women. It is not considered a sinister magical implement, because it serves only to increase the fortuneteller's ability to concentrate and helps with visualization.

Those who are so gifted and can see the past and future with the help of a crystal ball (or other transparent surface) follow a certain proceedure. The environment must be calm, one in which they will not be disturbed; a room that is nearly dark is ideal, with moonlight or a candle for illumination. The mind must be firmly focused on a certain person or question. With various magical hand movements, they transfer energy to the orb, and finally look into it with as much concentration as possible. After some time, multi-colored clouds appear in the ball or between the ball and viewer.

Interpretating what is seen

The clouds are interpreted in answer to the question asked based on the following pattern: ascending clouds are seen as a positive answer, sinking ones as a negative one. Their colors supply the viewer with additional information: black is unfavorable; white, favorable, success, good prospects; yellow is loss, unpleasant surprise, deceit; orange is disappointment, betrayal, slander; red is illness, danger, trouble of all kinds; violet, blue, and green: excellent, pleasant surprise.

Highly experienced crystal gazers claim they can even discern images in the crystal ball, which gradually provide a clear context for what is seen.

THE ART OF PROPHECY

History and origin

An oracle, for instance the prophesying Pythia, the priestess who resided over the Greek oracle at Delphi, is a divine revelation in the form of a phrase or a sign. The Pythia uttered her statements in a trance, inspired by the god Apollo, who foretold the future or made prophecies through her. In antiquity, oracles were bound to a place where petitioners could come. In Roman times there were augurs, people who interpreted omens based on the entrails of sacrificed

Pythia of Delphi once prophesied to a Persian king who wanted to conquer Greece that through his attack he would destroy a great empire. The king understood this to mean that he would be the victor of the war, but instead lost his own kingdom in the end.

animals or from the flight of birds. This was a widely accepted form of magical divination in many early high cultures, and was employed by Roman military leaders. To predict the outcome of a battle and to plan appropriate battle tactics, they studied the behavior of special fowl that had been brought along for that purpose.

Christianity as an obstacle for prophets

As Christianity spread in Europe, the art of prophecy was increasingly displaced in favor of Christian beliefs. On the other hand, numerous references to augury in Christian writings and the legends of saints testify to the fact that the art of bird prophecy continued in secret. Gregory the Great is said to have had pigeons whisper future events and mysteries into his ear. Legend has it Francis of Assisi could understand birds, meaning he had the gift of prophecy, an art still practiced by many primitive people today, and not only them: prophets are very popular in the Western world as well, even if their prophecies are frequently dubious.

After ritual preparation, the Pythia sat in the temple at Delphi and was overtaken by the god Apollo, who prohesied through her. Today we know that she fell into a trance from vapors seeping through a crevice at that spot, and priests probably whispered the words to her.

The exact origin of tarot cards remains unclear. It is generally accepted that they appeared with the arrival of migratory people in Europe in the thirteenth century, who were thought to come from India.

TAROT – THE ART OF LAYING AND READING CARDS

History and origin

The famous tarot, which has become increasingly popular in recent years, consists of seventy-eight cards. Of those, twenty-two are the major (or greater) arcana and fifty-six are minor arcana. The origin of the cards remains unclear. It is thought that Tarot spread through Europe in the thirteenth century with the arrival of migratory people. It is also a historical fact that the cards were prohibited in the city of Bern, Switzerland in 1367. Ten years later the cards emerged in Florence under the name *naibbe* or *naibbi*, which translates as "the center of the wheel" in Sanskrit.

The occultist Gérald Analect Vincent Encausse, called Papus (1865–1916), was convinced that tarot hearkened all the way back to ancient Egypt and transmitted the secret knowledge of the priesthood. In this vein, *ta* translated as "path" in ancient Egyptian, and *ro* as king; thus tarot would mean "path of the kings" or "the royal path."

The Rider-Waite deck

The oldest surviving deck is the Marseilles deck, which probably dates to the year 1760. The most commonly used version, however, is the Rider-Waite deck created by Arthur Edward Waite in 1910. The cards were drawn by Pamela Smith. Waite belonged to The Order of the Golden Dawn, and his cards are based on the works of Eliphas Levi (1810–1875), a French magus and author who is considered the founder of modern occultism (see pages 70 ff). In general, Waite followed the pattern of older cards, describing his tarot as "amended." Aleister Crowley (1875–1947) produced his own tarot deck, which was dedicated to the Egyptian god Thoth, in the 1940s. Crowley's interpretation draws on the Tree of Life known from the Kabbalah—the ten sephiroth, or the emanations of God (see pages 40 ff).

Major and minor arcana

The Latin word *arcana* is the plural of *arcanum*, "the secret." The major arcana consist of twenty-two trump cards numbered 0 to 21, each with their own name and image (the chariot, the tower, the world, etc.). The minor arcana consist of fourteen cards, ten number cards and four court cards (king, queen, knight, and page), in each of four suits. Usually, the twenty-two major arcana are used in fortunetelling and esoteric inauguration. Many magicians and esoterics consider the twenty-two major arcana to represent archetypes.

What are archetypes?
According to psychologist C.G. Jung (1875–1961), archetypes are "ancient pictures" or "ancient symbols" that arise from the collective unconscious and reflect the dreams of people of all cultures and times. These archetypes contain the collective (shared) experience of humankind. Archetypes can be brought into consciousness through the use of the tarot and its interpretation. Tarot cards thus make a connection between the conscious and the subconscious. For those who are familiar with tarot, this is nothing more than a stimulation of possibilities that are hidden within us, which can be drawn from the depths of the self and brought to light through the twenty-two major arcana. There are various instructions for achieving this.

The fifty-six minor arcana are divided into passive/even (goblets or cups and pentacles or coins) and active/odd (wands and swords) and assigned colors corresponding to signs of the zodiac or months. The four pictures are interpreted as basic magical symbols. For example, wands are assigned the element fire and the zodiac signs Aries, Leo, and Sagittarius; goblets correspond to the element air and the signs Gemini, Libra, and Aquarius.

The multicolored, magical tarot cards were mentioned by name for the first time in Florence, Italy. Some researchers suggest that they originated in ancient Egypt, because their name (*ta ro*) can be translated as "way of the kings."

Tarot in practice

In tarot, the cards drawn (either four, six, or ten) are laid out according to certain patterns that allow questions posed by the questioner to be answered. In the cross system, the cards are shuffled by a reader until the questioner, who wants to know about him- or herself and/or the future, stops the shuffling. The reader draws four cards, lays them face up in a cross before them, and then uses the following schema:

Card 1 (right): That is your subject or question.
Card 2 (left): You should not to do that.
Card 3 (above): That is the way.
Card 4 (below): This is where it leads (future).

The Rider-Waite deck from 1910 is the most famous tarot deck of modern times. It was drawn by Pamela Smith, who died completely impoverished in London. Arthur Edward Waite belonged to the Order of the Golden Dawn.

Recognizing your own potential

The procedure described above is the simplest and most frequently played variant, which even fortune-tellers also rely on. The idea underlying the use of the tarot for soothsaying is that a person's future is already known to his or her subconscious. Tarot readings thus serve only to help reveal what is already present. Similarly, all the potential developments that are within a person can be discerned through the unconscious drawing of cards and their interpretation. The respective meaning of each individual card is fixed, but the goal of reading tarot cards is to figure out what it means for a particular questioner. Card 13, Death, does not mean the physical demise of the questioner, but a radical new beginning, a reorientation. The Hanged Man card stands for perfect dedication, the acceptance of one's own fate.

Odin, the highest god of the Teutons, was considered a master of rune magic. According to the Old Norse legend collection Edda, he invented runes when he was wounded and hanging on a tree.

RUNE MAGIC

History and origin

Runes are Germanic characters known to have been used from the second century until the end of the nineteenth century across Europe—from Iceland to Romania and from the Baltic to the Mediterranean. Runes were not originally used as an alphabet, but were cut or engraved as symbols into wood, bone, metal, and stone. The origin of the runes remains unclear. The series of related alphabets known as Futhark are named after the first six letters: F U TH A R K.

The magic of runes

Runic characters can be found on weapons and amulets, on which each individual rune is not just a letter, but also represents an associated term, which is of particular importance in magical texts. A series of three T runes (Tyr runes), for example, are interpreted as a threefold repetition of the name Tyr, the old Germanic God of war. Naming Tyr twice is recommended when carving "victory runes;" cutting the F rune (Fehu rune) three times promised abundant possessions and wealth. In black magic, the R (Raido rune) is used, as it provides the triple meaning of dishonor, madness, and restlessness. Odin is the god of rune magic. A person who could carve and inscribe the best runes was considered a rune master. Even today, many people are attracted by the magical symbols and wear jewelry in the shape of a rune as a talisman or amulet.

This bronze figure from the ninth century probably depicts a priest of the god Odin. Those who ascribed to the powerful god of magic engraved runes to counter sickness and death, but also to harm others.

Thor, Odin's son, defended both gods and humans against evil forces, and even giants feared him. His hammer was his most important weapon in battle.

Runic alphabets

In Norse mythology, the god Odin, or Wotan, invented the magical runes during a period of self-sacrifice in which he spent nine nights wounded and suspended from a tree without food or drink. There are three runic alphabets: Germanic (or Elder) Futhark consists of twenty-four characters, Anglo-Saxon Futhark of twenty-nine, and Scandinavian (or Younger) Futhark has just sixteen symbols.

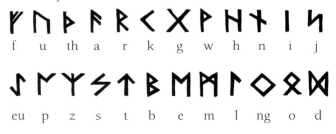

The Germanic Futhark consists of twenty-four runes.

An example of modern rune magic

You can make your own runes or buy them in amulet form in specialty stores. Runes made of an earthbound metal such as tin are best, as they are receptive to the energies of this "Earth ritual."

The rune magic is carried out in four steps:
1. **Purificatio (cleansing):** Before the runes are charged with energy, they are covered with salt and kept in a safe place overnight. This purifies them of any previous energy vibrations.
2. **Preparatio (preparation):** It is very important not to be interrupted or disturbed during a reading. When that is assured, darken the space, cover a table with a white tablecloth, and set out incense, a white candle, and a compass. In Norse thought, the Earth's strength flows from the north; therefore sit at the

table facing north, with the help of the compass. Then place the candle and incense in the middle of the table, light them, and place the runes near both of them.

3. **Potestatem facere (giving permission, charging):** With closed eyes, meditate for several minutes on the meaning of the runes while holding your hands held over them. Then visualize the following: the power of your own thoughts extends from the head, over the shoulders, through the arms and hands into the runes, then deeper through the Earth, into its interior, through the realms of roots and rocks, until it reaches deeply into the very core of Mother Earth. The fiery force of the element earth should be tangible; draw this into your own body. As soon as you feel warmth in your arms and hands, begin to touch the runes. While again focusing on the meaning of the runes, the earth energy is transferred to them until it finally disappears completely from your body.

4. **Salvatio (reconnection):** After the ritual is completed, take a few moments to recover and perhaps eat something light to help your body fully return to this world.

The healing power of runes

Some people believe that runes can help treat certain diseases. It should be noted, however, that medical effectiveness has not yet been proven.

FEHU	Eases breathing difficulties
THURISAZ	Improves heart problems
ANSUZ	Relieves mouth and tooth complaints
RAIDO	Soothes leg problems
JERA	Soothes digestive disturbances
EIHWAZ	Helps eye disease
ALGIZ	Combats insanity/headache
DAGAZ	Soothes anxiety, melancholy
LAGUZ	Eases disease of the renal system and urinary tract

The Vikings valued Thor's power and strength, as well. Stones of theirs are decorated with symbols that include both Odin and the Christian cross, in addition to the swastika.

A shaman is an intermediary between this life and the spirit worlds.
During a trance, his body becomes the workplace of gods and spirits.

SHAMANISM –
FLIGHT INTO OTHER WORLDS

What is a shaman?

A shaman is an intermediary between this world and
other realms, or the hereafter. Shamans are also healers
who believe that our present existence, our everyday
reality, is determined by "transintelligible" powers,
powers beyond human conception, though not outside
the realm of the soul!

A shaman often recognizes his or her gift following
unique experiences that may include signs, dreams,
visions, or health crises. An initiation ritual is generally
followed by years of further learning. Depending upon
the needs of their community, shamans offer their
powers as a helpful mediator while in a state of ecstasy
or a trance. Shamans served important religious functions in the archaic cultural world of hunters and
gatherers—a culture that existed long before the
emergence of high religions with their priestly
mediators, prophets, and reformers.

About the origin of the word

The Tungusic word *shaman* seems to be something
of a foreign word for the Tungu people native to Siberia
and Mongolia, as its meaning to them cannot be clearly
stated. Its origin has not been clarified. Shamans in
their classical, basic form can be found among many
peoples in the Eurasian area, particularly in Siberia.
There are also shamans in North and South America,
Oceania, Australia, and Africa. Regional manifestations
of shamanism are numerous.

Additional schamanistic elements are also components of the rituals of some high religions, for example, in exorcism, incantations, in baptism and wedding rituals, in connection with illness and death, as well as when blessing cattle and the harvest. Shamanism is an important basis of almost any magical practice, and above all astral projection.

The shaman's tools: drum, rattle, mask

A shaman usually has very specific implements: a drum or rattle, as well as certain articles of clothing, are essential elements of shamanic rituals. The clothing must be made from the fur or leather of certain animals and fabricated using special instruments. Additional articles of clothing might also be required, depending on where the shaman's journey takes them. The clothing may be painted with colored geometrical patterns and symbols (animals, sun, moon, stars, etc.). Often it is adorned with bells, fringes, pieces of metal, chains, or masks, which are representative of the shaman's protective spirits. The shaman wears a special headpiece, a metal antler-like helmet, or feathers on their head. Almost every aspect of the shaman's clothing represents their connection with the spirit world.

The meaning of the drum

Many objects play a role in shamanic rituals, including scarves, rope, parts of animals, candles, and musical instruments (drums, rattles, stringed instruments,

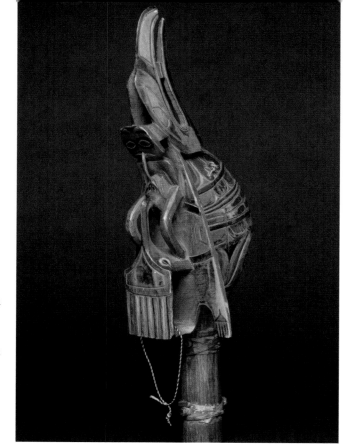

The shaman's personal protective spirit is his or her most important guide. This spirit is "found" during the shaman's initiation. Often it is the spirit of a predecessor, whose role they must soon take over.

bells). The most important instrument of the shaman, however, is the wooden drum. It is the vehicle for his journey, becoming his animal to ride, whether it be a horse, bird, or reindeer. The drum represents the protective spirit and is the materialized carrier of shamanic power.

Crafting the drum and bringing it to life is an important part of the journey to becoming a shaman. This includes looking for a suitable tree (often a birch or larch), acquiring the wood without killing the tree, creating the drum's form (round, egg-shaped, oval, etc.), and covering it with the skin of a certain animal. These processes are all complex and holy acts. When a drum is consecrated, it acquires its powerful soul. Finally, in order to journey into higher realms it requires a high resting place, such as a stake, tree, or ladder.

While in an altered state of consciousness called ecstasy, the shaman experiences a spirit journey in which the soul separates from the body. The soul thus travels into the otherworld—the realm of the hereafter and the spirit world.

Protective and helping spirits

The shamans' personal protective spirit is their most important guide. This spirit is found, discovered, or acquired during the initiation novice shamans undergo. Often it is the spirit of a shamanic predecessor, whose function the initiate will take on. In hunter-gatherer cultures, the protective spirit often appeared in the form of an animal. This so-called "animal mother" is the embodiment of shamanistic power—a totemic connection of animal and human. Animals and human beings form a kinship, are related to one another, and can transform themselves into each other. The shamans and their protective spirits can consult helping spirits, which often take the form of animals as well, as needed. They can act as messengers and companions in battle.

Shamanic tasks

Of the shaman's many functions, healing diseases is one of the most distinguished. Shamans are spiritual healers of the soul, and they come into contact with spirits in the course of their healings.

The basic precondition for successful treatment is a precise diagnosis of the cause of suffering, which the shaman determines while in a state of ecstasy. This condition lets the shaman discern the causes of the illness and determine which therapeutic measures are most appropriate. Shamans understand most complaints as resulting from evil spirits entering the body of their patients: they must be recognized, evaluated, and exorcised through rituals.

Shamanic rituals frequently include ropes, parts of animals, candles and musical instruments such as rattles, drums or bells, as well as a variety of stones.

Healing illness is one of the functions of a shaman. Before an appropriate cure can be used, the shaman must identify the spirit that has entered the patient.

Illness and soul loss

At the same time, a shaman has to determine what weakened the patient enough to allow evil spirits access in the first place—such as a breach of taboo, or black magic by ill-wishing neighbors, sorcerers, or magicians. Serious diseases with impaired consciousness are usually interpreted as soul loss: a part of the soul has been taken, kidnapped, and the shaman must find it in the spirit world, retrieve it, and reunite it. To do so, he or she undertakes a journey to the otherworld while in a state of ecstasy—a dangerous journey to the realm where spirits and demons reign.

Power over spirits

Shamans soothe the spirits, humor them, trick them, or combat them. Their highly developed supernatural gifts enable them to find what has been lost, whether it be things, animals, or people who have lost their way. Shamans can look into the past and future, and can interpret dreams and signs.

During their initiation, a substantial aspect of shamanic ability comes to the fore: the transmission of power. This power, this force from within, allows shamans to be both servants of the non-human and supernatural, and simultaneously to confront them—a richly intense relationship. Shamans have influence and power over the spirits. Using the force of their will, they can command and steer spirits, cause them to appear and banish them. This is only possible, however, if their will is strong enough. When shamans send their soul on a journey, they detach from their body, leaving the body vulnerable to the spirits with all of their supernatural powers—a dangerous venture that has left some shamans quite literally out of their minds, or mad.

A voodoo priestess in the USA. Due to Christian influences, voodoo as practiced in America and the Caribbean differs from the original African beliefs in many ways.

Soul journey to other worlds

In a state of ecstasy, shamans take what are called soul journeys, in which the soul separates from the body and travels to realms other than the earthly one we all experience. The remaining soulless body may be occupied by its protective spirit, and available as a medium. After protracted drumming, singing, dancing, jumping, and calling of the spirits, which often lasts several hours, the shaman finally achieves the wild, ecstatic high point of the trance, which ends in motionlessness and physical rigidity.

Neoshamanism

In the 1970s, the books written by ethnologist Carlos Castaneda aroused worldwide enthusiasm for and curiosity about this subject. In his writings, Castaneda explained how he became a student of the Mexican magician and shaman Don Juan and was consecrated into the secrets of the magical practices of Native Americans of southern North America. The use of drugs such as peyote or mescalin played a central role, as shamans in his tribe used them to facilitate their journeys to the spirit world.

One of Castaneda's students, Florinda Donner, relates how to overcome our everyday consciousness in favor of one that is far more comprehensive in her book *The Witches Dream: A Healer's Way of Knowledge*. Donner claims that we have an "assemblage point" about 24 inches (60 cm) below our right shoulder blade that habitually influences our usual perception. Through shamanic experience, this "assemblage point" can be relocated, which opens up additional and completely new ranges of perception. Today's neoshamanism and "shaman workshops," however, often have little to do with the healing practices of genuine shamans.

Voodoo: offensive and defensive magic

The term voodoo is derived from the West African-Creole word *vodun* (fetish). A fetish is an object thought to have supernatural powers, and fetishism is the veneration of fetishes. Two distinct forms of fetishism can be distinguished. In dynamic fetishism, supernatural forces are attributed to inanimate objects, such as amulets and talismans. Spirits may be bound to a certain object, and in animistic fetishism objects thought to contain charmed spirits are used for ritual worship or magical practices. Voodoo magic as it has been transmitted from the descendants of the African slaves in the USA and Central America is thus based on faith in the power of demons. The serpent god Damballah, who is said to help repel or induce magical attacks, is particularly venerated. Representations of snakes and snakeheads are extremely widespread in the voodoo cult. In addition, voodoo priests (houngan or hungan) and priestesses (mambo) are able to call upon the dead in order to consult them. In Haiti, voodoo has achieved equal footing with established religions.

Fearsome zombies and love charms

In Haiti, in particular, the fear of becoming a zombie after death is widespread, and there are countless horror stories about zombies sent into the fields to

Santeria magic in Cuba
It is not only Marxism that flourishes in Fidel Castro's Cuba, but also an old world of magical belief—Santeria, or Regla de Ocha, the most widespread religious practice in Cuba. It has its roots in Africa, especially among the Yoruba, the origin of many Cubans. Santeria is based on ritual worship of the Orisha divinities, which are mythological figures associated with certain natural elements as well as symbolic attributes, colors, and gender. Ochún is the santo of love and prosperity, Changó the spirit of thunder, and Yemayá is ruler of the oceans as well as the great primary mother. These divinities speak to humans through different oracles or possess people during religious ceremonies, through whom they convey messages.
Santeros—or their female counterparts, Santeras—can be recognized by their white garb. They are open to everything, and it generally causes no conflict with their religious beliefs to read the oracle or demonstrate dancing and singing for tourists for a few dollars. Objects that have magical meaning for Santeria can be found in many shops in Havana, including Kauri shells to help predict the future and herbs that help to drive away evil spirits as well as with affairs of the heart. Most Santeria high priests, called babalawos, live in the harbor area of Havana, considered the center of Santeria in Cuba.

work endlessly, with no will. According to Haitian beliefs, zombies are living dead who have been roused by thorn apple poison, but have no will of their own, and thus remain under the control of their masters. The unscrupulous voodoo priests who revive them put zombies to work as slaves. One can supposedly recognize a zombie by its blank facial expression.

Voodoo magicians also use love charms; they allegedly know how to call forth a suitable beloved for anyone, one who will match their wishes and criteria for an ideal partner.

Voodoo is frequently viewed as a form of black magic, which is at least partly due to the fact that voodoo priests communicate with the deceased.

Magicians protect themselves from encroachment by the beings they summon during rituals by drawing a circle or a magical triangle. The circle above demarcates the protected zone, which supernatural beings may not enter.

SPELLS – INVOCATIONS OF POWER

The power of words

From "Open Sesame!" in *Ali Baba and the Forty Thieves* to "abracadabra" or "simsalabim," the idea behind every magical phrase is that certain words can be so powerful that they produce material consequences. The magic word "abracadabra" was already used in antiquity to fight disease. Its magical power was thought to unfold to its fullest when it was written eleven times, underneath each other, with one letter omitted each time:

Abrakadabra
Abrakadabr
Abrakadab
Abrakada
etc.

Other examples of spells and magical words from antiquity and the Middle Ages are:

Alohomora — opens doors
Baddiwasi — cleans keyholes
Dissendium — opens secret passages
Expelliarmus — disarms opponents
Finite incantem — ends a ritual
Peskiwichtli Pesternomi— brings depravity and downfall
Rictussempra — produces the feeling of being tickled

Practical procedure

The practice of invocation ultimately consists of nothing more than the realization of a divine or demonic image, an image that the magician must imprint in their mind and visualize in great detail, reconstructing it before one's spiritual eye. This becomes increasingly difficult with more abstract spirits and demons. Many celestial beings—for example Bael, who teaches how one can become invisible—are known only as geometrical forms. That level of abstraction makes it all the more important to know the name of the one being summoned, as their name signifies their essential self.

The white-robed Druids of the British Isles met on certain days of the year at Stonehenge, including the equinoxes, where they used magical rituals and dances to glorify the forces of nature and the cosmos.

Vibration of the voice

Invocation is accompanied by visualization: the name is articulated with a deep, clear, and most importantly, vibrating voice. Vibration is used to rouse the magical abilities in the depths of our consciousness. The letters that spell the name are visualized, as well. Strictly speaking, an invocation is a deep prayer, a mantra, e.g.: Hare Krishna, Hare Krishna, Krishna, Krishna, Hare, Hare, Hare Rama, Hare Rama, Rama, Rama, Hare Krishna. The tone of the voice not only purifies the consciousness and releases it from disturbing influences, but also grants one power over the summoned being.

The opposite of the invocation is an **evocation**, in which the magician assumes that the spirit being conjured is to be found outside of the body.

The powerful curses of the Druids

In Ireland there were women who, for a fee, would approach someone deserving of malediction, stand firmly planted before them, and deliver their curse—often before a curious crowd. But their forerunners, the Druids, also knew how to deliver devastating curses.

The Druids, the white-robed Celtic priestly class of the British Isles, were masters of the curse. Druidic curses only rarely missed their mark; people widely believed in their power. They possessed great knowledge of nature, and also understood psychological techniques they could use to impress more ignorant people, sometimes even driving them to death. According to reports of several Roman authors, thanks to their powers of suggestion, the Druids often managed to achieve their goals, even among the Romans.

Invocations

An invocation is a summoning of demons or spirits, who then appear to the magician in order to assist with his or her magic activities. The most important ability for effective invocations is the imagination, which must be trained to visualize forms and symbols with great clarity and precision. Magicians of the Order of the Golden Dawn relied on the assistance of ancient Egyptian gods such as Isis or Osiris in their practices.

Isis, the great goddess, restores Osiris to life.

The Celtic Druids were masters of persuasion and malediction, and enjoyed high regard as a result.

Glam dicin, the most dangerous curse

One of the curses at the disposal of the Celtic Druids was called "glam dicin." A powerful form of magic that invoked forces of chaos, it was directed against those who had broken a contract or were guilty of murder. The widely feared curse that "no herb could counter" sickened or even killed its victim.

According to legend, there is one known case when the curse failed. A female Druid who had fallen in love with a man placed a destructive curse on him: if he should leave her, he would die on the same day. The man, however, loved another woman—what could be done? Was there some way to remove the curse? When he accidentally injured the Druidess and sucked on her wound, she lost her power over him. This was because, according to Celtic beliefs, they had become blood relations and thus could no longer share table and bed.

Magical rites and spells to bring good luck

Spells and magical procedures often follow strange patterns that at first glance might seem incredibly odd.

In order to attract luck and ward off misfortune, for example, one code of magical practice recommends wearing a few pieces of clothing inside out. This is most effective during a waxing moon, which is regarded as the best time for conducting magic anyway, since spells cast then bring the best results. Light a candle a say the following words aloud three times: "I will experience happiness and success everywhere and at all times." Try it!

The notorious dragon breath, a harmful spell

If someone is spreading false rumors about you, the following ritual from the treasure trove of magic spells should help. The spell requires something sweet (candies or chocolates), a clove of garlic, a green candle and a beautifully decorated dish:

1. Put the candy in the dish and place it on a windowsill so that the contents are illuminated by the moon's light.
2. Light the candle and place it alongside the dish.
3. Take the garlic and use it to draw an imaginary circle around the dish. Say out loud: "Whoever is spreading bad rumors should have breath to match."

4. Blow out the candle—this "grounds" the magic.
5. Offer the rumormonger one of the enchanted candies.

The effects are supposed to be overwhelming!

Sympathetic magic

The magical thinking of the Teutons and other peoples was informed by specific symbolic relationships within the magical practices used. Wild animals that stood out for qualities such as strength, speed, and wildness were preferred over gentler creatures, for example. Male animals were thought to be stronger than the females. Patients yellowed by jaundice were given earthworms with "yellow rings" to eat. The earthworms were chopped into such small pieces, however, so that the patients remained unaware of what they were eating. Sympathetic magic essentially works with the principle of similarity, meaning that qualities can be transferred to something similar in order to heal or strengthen it. The bark from the east side of a tree was ascribed special power, for instance, as it was illuminated by

the rising sun but not by the setting sun. A triple curse is said to shrink an abcess—one thing corresponds with the other: "You should be consumed like wood in the oven. Shrink like a cow pie on the wall. Evaporate like water in the bucket!" (4)

Minerals as magic stones

Sympathy means "attraction," in contrast to antipathy ("repulsion"). The occultist Agrippa (1486–1535) refined the old system of sympathetic magic. Regarding the effects of minerals, he explained that jasper at a birthing helps to bring the baby. Amethyst, the gemstone on the rings worn by Catholic bishops, wards off drunkenness and is thus "antipathetic," while bringing blessings and happiness at the same time. Homeopathy ultimately returns to the ancient doctrine of signatures, treating like with like—one of its central principles.

Purple amethyst is the gemstone on the ring traditionally worn by Catholic bishops. As a stone that brings blessings, it promotes good luck and health. In antiquity, people also believed that it prevented drunkenness.

TEACHERS OF MAGIC

Many people consider the Englishman Aleister Crowley to be the founder of modern Satanism. He himself furthered his reputation as the Antichrist.

ALEISTER CROWLEY
THE GODLESS MAGICIAN

Childhood, youth, apprenticeship

Aleister Crowley took great pleasure in describing himself as "the wickedest man in the world," and is regarded, especially by the Church, as the "father of modern Satanism." For many people of faith, Crowley—who was born in 1875 in a small, unremarkable town close to Stratford-upon-Avon, Shakespeare's birthplace—embodied the Antichrist, especially because of the sexual magic practices he engaged in, which he publicly flaunted. Crowley's father was a wealthy master brewer, and his mother a "brainless bigot," according to her son.

His parents raised Aleister with puritanical strictness, which may be one reason why his favorite readings were from the Book of Revelation. Two things bound young Crowley to this apocalyptic text, which describes the end of the world: the tantalizing whore of Babylon, dressed in purple and scarlet (later the magician routinely felt drawn to women who wore those colors) and the beast 666, the animal of the apocalypse, which rose from the sea and with whom Crowley himself identified. The beast 666 possessed the power to war against everything holy and to triumph. Young Aleister decided that he wanted to be able to do that, too.

Crowley's father died of tongue cancer when he was 11, and his mother disowned her sinful son after she caught him with a servant girl. At age 20, Crowley began to study the humanities at Cambridge University. He wrote poems, climbed mountains, and during his university years came into contact with the Secret Order of the Golden Dawn (see pages 85 ff). This society's practice of magical rituals deeply impressed the then 23-year-old Aleister.

The pentagram ritual

Crowley was especially impressed by the pentagram ritual used to conjure spirits and deities. From 1899 he lived in a small apartment in London, focusing solely on spiritual exercises—with the help of drugs, among other things. He called himself a magician, and he wanted to be one who embodied everything sinister associated with the word. He is said to have induced people to crawl about on their hands and knees and howl like dogs. In 1900 Crowley retreated to Scotland in order to experiment with dangerous rituals, with the express goal of winning greater power over other people.

The magic Abbey of Thelema

Later, as his popularity (or notoriety) as a magician was at its height, Crowley took on nothing less than the creation of a new age: Aion. In 1920, he founded the Abbey of Thelema on Sicily. Here men and women should find and follow their true will. "Do what you want, and never fear that a god will punish you for it!" was the only law of this community, which viewed magic as a method for developing one's true self. The will of the individual should be strengthened and the body sensually experienced.

In 1920, Crowley founded the Abbey of Thelema on the island of Sicily, which was closed three years later by the state.

Crowley published announcements in New York newspapers in which he sought humpbacked, one-eyed, and lame women in order to transform them into well-formed, beautiful women at Thelema. This is how the magician found some of his lovers, many of whom were likely devoted to him for life because of his sadomasochistic disposition. In 1923, Mussolini closed the abbey because not only small animals, but also children, had allegedly been sacrificed there. Also, a visitor collapsed and died during a ceremony in which a cat was killed and its blood imbibed.

Aleister Crowley with his first wife, Rose Kelly. Appearances can be deceiving: not long after the wedding she began to drink because he treated her so badly, and she finally left him in order to be free again.

soon considered the most experienced of all. In 1909 Crowley divorced once more, in order to be free for as many partners as possible. It cannot be denied that Aleister Crowley was highly attractive to a large number of women—perhaps because he was so animalistic and enjoyed playing the devil.

Magic systems and final years

In the magical system developed by Crowley—a mixture of number mysticism and ancient Greek and Egyptian magic—one could supposedly heighten one's concentration through endless repetition of specific formulas, which eventually led to a deep meditative state. Through this procedure, one could achieve mastery of one's body in order to stop feeling pain, for example.

In 1929 Crowley married Maria Teresa Ferari in Leipzig. They spent some years together in Berlin until Crowley grew weary of her. Visitors to the two did not give only flattering reports: the strange occultist had become fat, was dressed in bizarre clothing, and was surrounded by a cloud of perfume. He had shaved his head bald and his gaze was still penetrating. The best-known magician in Europe, by that time addicted to heroin and gravely ill, died in 1947 in a castle near Hastings, shortly after he had developed a new deck of tarot cards. "I am surprised" are said to have been his last words.

The "Beast's" tarot cards

Crowley, who was dubbed "the Beast" because of his enormous sexual appetite and avowed enmity toward Christianity, created a new and fascinating tarot deck. Many scholars assume the origins of tarot to have been ancient Egypt or even the sunken Atlantis (see pages 48 ff). Tarot cards appeared for the first time in Italy around 1300. Over time, different versions of the deck have been used as an illustrated oracle, most of them in the style of Anne-Marie Lenormand, a famed card reader of Napoleon's time. Crowley based his version of tarot on the tradition of the Egyptian god Thoth, the great god of magic, and called it "The Book of Thoth." Crowley's tarot is psychologically aligned; the surreal,

Marriage and founding of the Order

Aleister Crowley traveled to Japan, India, and Egypt; in 1903 he married Rose Kelly, who bore him a daughter one year later. Crowley gave his daughter the symbolic name Nut Ma Ahthoor Hecate Sappho Jezebel Lilith.

Over the course of the following years, Crowley wrote nineteen books about magic and occultism. In 1907 he founded the AA Order (Argenteum Astrum/ Silver Star), for which he recruited twenty-eight members. This order specialized in the teachings of sexual magic practices, in which the magician was

Crowleys long years of excessive drug and alcohol use left their marks.
He died in 1947, addicted to heroin, in Hastings, England.

multicolored pictures are supposed to reveal to the questioner his or her deepest, innermost self.

Kabbalah and visions

Crowley regarded it as his life's work to change the general opinion of tarot as merely fortunetelling play. He attempted to do this by connecting tarot cards with the Kabbalah (see pages 40 ff).

A twist of fate brought Crowley into contact with the highly gifted artist Lady Frieda Harris in 1937. Goal-oriented meditation and magical rituals brought him visions of a new tarot deck, which he sketched onto paper and which Lady Frieda Harris then perfected.

Crowley wrote an instructional book to accompany the cards, which clarified their use. Crowley's order, the Ordo Templi Orientis (O.T.O.), first published the work privately in 1944 in an edition of 200 copies.

ELIPHAS LEVI
THE SEARCH FOR THE KEYS

Magic, the queen of society

The Frenchman Alphonse Louis Constant (1809–1875), who later called himself Eliphas Levi, is considered the leading occultist of the nineteenth century. Along with Aleister Crowley, he is among the outstanding magicians of modern times. Materialism was in its first bloom during Levi's time, and people who studied magical knowledge did not enjoy high regard. But Eliphas Levi disregarded mockery and scorn—he was determined to record the history of magic in its entirety. In his work *Transcendental Magic, its Doctrine and Ritual*, he began with the origin of occult philosophy and attempted to illuminate hermetic teachings.

Magic as a specialized language

Eliphas Levi, trained as a Catholic priest, was a very ambitious person who was determined to restore magic to its true importance. He tried to point out that the magical, symbolic language once served as a legitimate specialized language—just like the current specialized languages of medicine or law. He maintained that "once" referred to a general time period in ancient Egypt and in ancient Mesopotamia, the land of two rivers on the Euphrates and Tigris.

The lost magical keys

Levi wanted to revitalize the magical knowledge of earlier times. He spoke about "magical keys" which had supposedly been lost. Rediscovering those keys would reveal all the mysteries of the world. First, he equated the twenty-two major arcana of the tarot (magician, high priest, ruler, emperor, pilgrim, etc.) with the twenty-two letters of the Hebrew alphabet. In the Kabbalah there are twenty-two forces of creation (the letters of the alphabet), which function like an antenna to harness the universal energies and make them useful. Visualizing the relevant signs furthered this process. Visualization means forming a mental image of something in order to join it with a specific desire. In this way, writing, speaking and visualization of the three following Hebrew letters—סאל—every day ensure a secure financial situation, as well as a debt-free life. Eliphas Levi must be given credit for establishing the connection between the Hebraic Kabbalah as a magical form with the tarot, which probably developed around 1300 in Italy.

The Frenchman Eliphas Levi is considered to have paved the way for modern occultism. This is one of the reasons Aleister Crowley regarded himself as Levi's reincarnation, as he was born only a few months following Levi's death.

Hermes Trismegistos

Hermetic philosophy is said to have been founded by the great Hermes Trismegistos (literally, "Hermes thrice great"). At least two Mediterranean divinities merge in this figure: Thot, the Egyptian god of magic, and Hermes, founder of alchemy. The Greek poet Homer narrates that Hermes Trismegistos lived long before the pharoahs. No less than 20,000 magical texts are attributed to him. Among them is the *Tabula Smaragdina* (*Emerald Tablet*), well-known in the Occident. It begins with the famous lines: "What is below is like that above, and that above like that below, to accomplish the miracles of the One." For alchemists, the *Emerald Tablet* is of the utmost significance, as it demonstrates that the material and spiritual worlds permeate one another, and are one. Hermes Trismegistos is named at the beginning of all written magical revelations, and all Western magical literature refers to him.

Hermetic philosophy is thought to have been founded by the great Hermes Trismegistos. Two divinities are merged in him: Thot, the Egyptian god of magic, and Hermes, the founder of alchemy.

Eliphas Levi was a very ambitious man whose goal was to return magic to its original significance. He wanted to demonstrate that the magical language of symbols once served as a legitimate specialized language, in ancient Egypt, for example.

The conjuring of Apollonius of Tyana

In June 1854, Levi successfully performed a necromancy ritual. With the help of the pentagram ritual, he conjured the spirit of Apollonius of Tyana, who was active as a magician and philosopher in the Roman Empire in the first century AD. What arrived from the realm of the dead was reportedly an emaciated, sad-looking man in a gray robe, who emanated nothing but chill. He disappeared once more, without speaking, as Levi was close to fainting. "The apparition did not speak with me at all, but it seemed as if the questions I had wanted to ask it were answered in my most inner self." (7) Shortly before his death, Eliphas Levi returned to the fold of his mother church: "The truth does not come to an end, but our dreams do," he wrote in *A History of Magic*.

Do the souls of the cremated snatch young girls?

Demons and possession today?
Duma, India, January 2006: The director of a school in Madhya Pradesh asked a magician for assistance in fighting demons that had afflicted exclusively the female students for the past week. Both the teachers of the school and the parents of the girls hoped that spiritual purification rituals would bring the unsettling activities to an end. The reason for the appearance of the demons is thought to be the school's location, as the building was constructed on the site of a former crematorium. The local Hindu priest, Uma Shastri, is also convinced that the souls of the cremated could not find any peace and had taken possession of the bodies of the girls. It should also be mentioned that the teenagers fell into a trance, danced around wildly, and were not in possession of their senses.

In June of 1854, Levi successfully used necromancy to summon the ghost of Apollonius of Tyana, who was a magician and philosopher in the Roman Empire in the first century AD.

DION FORTUNE
WITCH AND WISE WOMAN

The life and work of a modern witch

Dion Fortune certainly led a very unusual life. She was born as Violet Firth in 1890 in London. In 1946, she died of leukemia in the same city. In 1919, she joined the famous secret society The Golden Dawn, which she was soon forced to leave, however, as her opinions were too radical for Moina McGregor Mathers, the leader of the order. Violet Firth changed her name to Dion Fortune as she entered the Order of the Golden Dawn. The name was based on her family's motto, *deo nun fortuna*, which roughly translates as "by God and not by destiny."

Dion Fortune wanted to be a real witch, not one who cheated her audience with table tricks, but one who possessed true and independent, God-given power. Her experiences and studies led her to form an esoteric circle, the Fraternity of the Inner Light, which still exists today as the Society of the Inner Light, and follows Fortune's knowledge and modern hermetic teachings. Dion Fortune's books, *The Mystical Qabalah* (1935) and especially *The Cosmic Doctrine* (1920), claim to reveal the highest levels of the Egyptian mysteries as well as numerous occult teachings and the secrets of moon magic.

Dion Fortune was born Violet Firth in London, England in 1890 and died of leukemia in the same city in 1946. In 1919, she joined the famous secret society, The Golden Dawn, which she soon left.

Moon magic

The different phases of the moon as they relate to magical practices play an important role among all ancient societies of the Earth. It is commonly believed that spells and rituals are most effective during specific phases of the moon, for example, healing magic about three days before or after a full moon. In the cult of Wicca, modern witchcraft, the "moon goddess" is prayed to and honored in cult ritual.

Struggles on the astral level

Dion Fortune's self-confident appearances in the Order of the Golden Dawn did not remain without consequences. Moira McGregor Mathers not only insulted the young witch, but also tried to fight her on the astral level, Dion Fortune writes. This reminds one of shamanistic activity and powerful enchantresses of tales and legends.

The witch described what such an astral battle looked like as follows: "As I was lying in bed one afternoon, I was overwhelmed by thoughts of revenge and therefore unable to sleep. The old Nordic myths rose again before my eyes, and there was Fenris, the

During one of her astral journeys, Dion Fortune met Fenris, a wolf monster from the Nordic myths. It materialized from ectoplasma directly beside her in bed.

wolf monster. At the same moment I felt a strange pulling on my sun network, and soon a large gray wolf materialized next to me on the bed. It was a well-materialized form of ectoplasma (an astral substance, which distinguishes the astral body on media)—gray and colorless, and it was heavy." (8)

Elements as weapons

Dion Fortune sensed the body of the magical wolf beside her, but succeeded in dissolving the astral body of the wolf again with the help of the visualization of a sort of "Jacob's ladder" leading from heaven to Earth. She also had the ability to create beings from her own ectoplasma with the "Jacob's ladder." She could see how such "elements" confronted hated enemies or how they fought against one another while in a state of trance. Lastly, a cat as large as a tiger appeared to her in the stairway, which she believed to be McGregor Mathers, or Vestigia (her magic name, or motto). They fought violently with one another. At the end, Dion's back was "covered with scratches, as though a cat had fallen upon her." (8)

Magical strength and concentration

One of Dion Fortune's books, in which one can read everything about the art of fighting on the astral level, is called *Psychic Self-Defense*. The main emphasis of the witch's books and of the Fraternity of the Inner Light, which she founded in Glastonbury, England, is how to develop magical powers. Every magician must understand him- or herself as their own guide—by God, not by destiny. The magician guides the power of the stars, not the other way around!

Dion Fortune understood God as an inexhaustible reservoir of power. Her motto was to concentrate on the divine substance within oneself. Faith, absolute will, and magical concentration help us achieve this. At the same time, the experiences that we all collect throughout our lifetime should activate and enable existing abilities.

Through visualization, the sorceress was able to create a sort of "Jacob's ladder," which led from heaven to Earth. In this way she

Magic takes practice and self-discipline

On this path to self-discovery, initiation ceremonies and magical rituals serve the purpose of bringing the unconscious into consciousness, and may produce powerful mental pictures, which are vividly imagined and enunciated. For Dion Fortune and every other magician, magic is and remains a question of perceiving the universe differently. This is achieved through self-discipline as a result of hard work improving oneself. Naturally, you have to master specific techniques, such as visualization, for example. Every kind of magic rests on the belief that strong visualization has genuine effects, because matter reacts to the power of thought. The idea that consciousness can form and influence matter is an important component of every sort of magic.

gained power over other beings from her own ectoplasma, which she set loose on hated enemies.

FRANZ BARDON AND HIS GREAT MAGICAL UNIVERSE

Life and work

The Czech Franz Bardon (1909–1959) developed a magical system from the secret teachings of various lodges (Freemasons, Rosicrucians, Illuminati), and combined his insights and elements of Eastern teachings such as Taoism and Tibetan occultism, for example. Bardon was one of the most important magicians and occultists of the twentieth century. His first book, *Initiation into Hermetics*, is especially notable for its emphasis on practicle and feasible exercises, and practice as the means to advancement. The avowed goal of this modern magician was to offer serious students of magic the very best training possible outside of an occult society or without the advantage of a personal tutor (which he agreed was optimal).

During the time of the Nazis, Bardon was imprisoned; he was cruelly tortured when he refused to put

Franz Bardon was the son of a Christian mystic. Although little is known about his childhood, it is assumed that his knack for the occult was already apparent in his early youth.

his magical powers at their disposal. After the war, Bardon continued with his studies of magic and wrote a total of four very successful books. Many of his ideas about the occult are inspired by the works of other magicians, such as those by Eliphas Levi or, although Bardon never mentioned it, Aleister Crowley's system of magic.

Love is the most important power in the universe

The mental exercises that Bardon prescribes, such as inner concentration and observing the wandering mind, can also be found in similar forms in yoga and

Bardon's teachings are essentially based on the four elements which were already known in antiquity: Fire, Earth, Air, and Water. He added a fifth, Quintessence, also called Akasha.

other forms of meditation. Although it is hard to imagine greater differences between Franz Bardon and Aleister Crowley—Bardon was an unassuming man and a pragmatic thinker, while Crowley tended toward megalomania—Crowley's influence is nonetheless clearly present. Crowley's slogan "Love is the law, love under will," is also the fundamental idea underpinning Bardon's worldview. It was also important for Bardon to make the elementary distinction between the consciousness of everyday life and "magical" consciousness absolutely clear to his students.

The strange "fluids"

Franz Bardon presupposed an energetic model of the universe modified in accordance with Eastern theories. He writes about "fluids" (intangible energy flows or forces): the "electrical" and the "magnetic" fluids are mutually complementary much like yin and yang, and are thus in agreement. According to Bardon, magnetism is a cool, negative force with a blue emanation, while electricity is a warm, positive force with a red emanation.

In his work *Initiation into Hermetics*, Bardon stated that every part of the human body is normally governed by these electric and magnetic powers, but can also be neutral. Neutral means that the electric and magnetic fluids perfectly balance or neutralize each other, which happens rarely among people. Illnesses occurs when the electric and magnetic fluids are out of balance.

The four elements

Bardon's cosmology is grounded on the four ancient elements—Fire, Earth, Air, and Water—in addition to "Akasha," or Quintessence, the fifth element. The term *Akasha* comes from Hindu philosophy and means something like "ether," meaning a subtle element, like an astral body. For the most part, Bardon associated the elements with the same human powers as other magicians: water stands for emotions and intuition, fire for aggression or passion, etc. From his point of view, the competent magician is one who is able to manipulate the elements to achieve the results he or she desires. A prerequisite for this level of mastery is for students to control and harmonize all the elements within their own being before they can become masters of the elements. The first step toward that is for each student to become conscious of all the individual elements within them, which takes place through magical training.

Among other things, Bardon studied the teachings and ways of the Freemasons, which became part of the magical system he developed.

The magician rules over spirits and demons

Bardon taught that humans, as tetrapolar beings that incorporate all four elements, are ranked above all spirits, demons, and angels—but only if we have united all four elements within ourselves. He discusses gnomes and sylphs, which are also called elements as examples. This teaching of elemental spirits originated with the doctor, magician, and philosopher Paracelsus

According to Paracelsus' teachings, fairies were also among the elemental spirits. In addition to dwarves, trolls, will-'o-the-wisps, and elves, they composed the group of earth spirits, or gnomes.

(1494–1541). For him, the gnomes were earth spirits who bestowed magical powers on the Earth, and sylphs were air spirits that resembled butterflies.

Bardon warned his students, just as Paracelsus had warned his, to be on their guard against the deceptions and tricks of the elemental spirits, who want to capture a part of the human soul. Bardon wrote, "Any deliberate cause, maybe such as a wish, a thought or any imagination created in this sphere together with the dynamic concentration of willpower, unshaken faith, and fullest conviction is bound to be realized with the help of the elements." (9)

In magic, human consciousness knows neither time nor space, and is therefore an Akasha principle, transcendent, independent of life and death and independent of the material world. For this reason, everything the magician longs for becomes visible. Because magicians must exert control over all the elemental spirits, the magician him or herself cannot be out of balance. All forms of obsession (including drugs or anything else that is addictive) can also lead students to fail eventually. For this reason, Bardon insisted that students beginning magical study undertake a rigorous and ruthlessly honest introspection over a number of weeks, in order to note one's own shortcomings and weaknesses. Magical work is first and foremost work on oneself and one's flaws.

The magic curriculum

Bardon divides his magical practices into ten stages, which at times seem somewhat arbitrary.

1. Self-analysis
As mentioned above, the first step in learning magic is the student's difficult and disciplined work in understanding the four elements in their own personality and harmonizing them within themself. Only after this can one begin occult work, according to Bardon. At the beginning, the initiate's virtues and strengths, as well as their errors and weaknesses, come to light.

2. Concentration and breathing exercises
The next step for students is to strengthen their ability to concentrate, and practice breathing exercises as well as the technique of autosuggestion (self-influence,

Bardon maintained that spiritual forces can be mobilized when a magician can simply activate his or her energies in a specific situation through a hand motion, or a silent formula. Thus the ocean might rise in response to a magician's command, for example.

strengthening the imaginative faculty). Bardon viewed this as the key to the subconscious. He distinguished between two forms of breathing: breathing with the lungs, and breathing through the skin. His thesis is that the body can breathe by itself, but it is essential for students to learn to control breathing. Both forms are combined in order to inhale the individual elements and Akasha.

3. Visualization exercises and manipulation of the elements

This stage of Bardon's training is concerned with intensive concentration and the visualization of increasingly complex objects. At the same time, students deepen their practice of "inhaling" the elements into the body. They also learn magical "loading" of areas or objects, for example to use in healing or for their own protection. Students become more adept at working with their own spiritual energy.

4. Control of magical energy through rituals

In Franz Bardon's magic system, rituals function as memory techniques, based on hand gestures, verbal formulas, or visual cues. He claimed that when an adept has truly understood the energies, he or she can activate their own energies in a specific situation simply through a hand motion, an unspoken formula, or a combination of both.

According to Bardon, levitation, which is the separation of the astral and physical bodies brought about through one's own will, is a prerequisite for making contact with the astral world. Levitation also means the ability to lift oneself into the air.

5. Transfer of consciousness and levitation

The fifth level consists of a series of exercises that prepare the magician for physical and astral levitation (the separation of the physical and astral bodies), in anticipation of making contact with astral beings. Magicians can communicate with the astral world actively or passively. Bardon found that passive techniques were easier and safer, and he thus presented them first.

6. Making contact with astral beings and taking astral journeys

In addition to astral beings and astral travel of one's astral body, controlled by the strength of one's will, this level of magical practice is also concerned with the creation of non-physical entities to be used by the magician. Bardon also discusses the great danger of an accidental creation of such a being. These phantasms can harm the magician. At this point, Bardon again stressed how important it is that students of magic do not omit any stage of their development to ensure that such dangers do not arise in the first place.

7. Prophecy and other abilities

Bardon recommended special aids such as eye-baths and earplugs, meant to facilitate the development of extrasensory perception abilities. He also thematized magical animation of pictures and statues via energy transfer.

8. Bardon's "fluid condensers"

Bardon used specific devices called "fluid condensers" to concentrate, store, and handle the electrical and magnetic "fluids." He supplied detailed instructions about how to create these condensers, and how they are "loaded" and used. He recommended preparing a tincture of gold in order to strengthen each condenser created by students of magic. This is achieved by dissolving 1 gram of soluble gold chloride in 20 grams of distilled water—an expensive undertaking.

An example of a condenser recipe from the master

Place a handful of fresh or dried chamomile flowers into a pan, then fill it with enough cold water to immerse them. Bring the water to the boil and let the flowers simmer for 20 minutes, then cool in the covered pan. Return the liquid (without the blossoms) to the heat and let it thicken until it weighs about 50 grams. This extract is preserved by mixing it with the same amount of alcohol, but not methyl alcohol. Then add about 10 drops of the gold tincture described above into the mixture. Bardon wrote, "If you wish to use the condenser for your own purposes, you may still strengthen it, by adding a drop of your blood or sperm, if possible both together, on a swab of cotton, throw this afterwards without any scruples into the condenser and shake it well. Then, pour all in a funnel, through filter paper or linen into a flask and keep it well corked in a cool and dark place to be ready for use." (9)

Gold has a strengthening effect on the fluid condensers. Bardon therefore advised preparing gold tinctures that can be combined with the various condensers.

The purpose of the condensers

In Bardon's own words: "The magician can use these condensers in many ways: mixing them with liquids to drink, for anointing, mixing them with incense compounds, or pouring them in small bowls to collect and concentrate certain energies.

Any fluid condenser which has been prepared in this manner does not lose its efficiency even after many years. The condenser must be well shaken each time you are going to use it, the bottle is to be corked again after withdrawing some out of it. In the same way you can prepare several universal condensers from Russian or genuine Chinese tea, from lily-blossoms—best are the white ones—popular leaves, alraune roots or mandragora roots, arnica montana, acacia flowers. Any simple fluid condenser, prepared from one plant, is sufficient for normal use such as influencing through the elements, or developing the astral senses by means of the fluid condensers." (9)

All of Bardon's books are characterized by the fact that they use relatively little theory and are easy to understand. They are practically organized and therefore classic grimoires—instructions for the independent practice of practical magic.

9. The use of magic mirrors

The magic mirror, like the crystal ball, plays a role in many magical practices. Following a short description, in this section Bardon described many examples of how magicians can use the mirror.

10. Elevating the spirit to higher spheres

Finally, Bardon discussed how students of magic can improve their spiritual qualities, with emphasis on self-discipline and daily practice. Bardon wanted to make clear that magic contributes to insight about oneself as much as to awareness of the various levels of the universe. Magic only becomes true power through love. Bardon's thesis can be summed up as follows: one who truly loves already has magical powers, which they can and should make use of in service of others.

Evocations or summoning demons

Bardon's second publication was a 500-page book entitled *The Practice of Magic Evocation*. It is an extraordinary and unparalleled book concerning communion with spirits, and a classical grimoire, referred to as a practical introduction along with magical handbooks by experts.

The first of the work's two parts describes in great detail the numerous aids and equipment that magicians require for their work: staff, sword, magic circle, lamp, triangle, incense burner, mirror, cap, trident, crown, etc.

In the second part of the book, Bardon introduced a very extensive compendium of spirits and beings that students of magic should be able to contact once they have perfected the techniques of evocation. In evocation, "lower" spirits and demons are summoned, which is in contrast to invocation, in which one conjures the higher range of demons, spirits, and angels (see pages 60 ff).

Names of spirits and demons

Bardon briefly described most beings according to their special skills and abilities: what knowledge can they share, or what use can they be to the conjurer? Bardon repeatedly claimed that he had contacted each of these beings himself and that he was describing them from first-hand experience. The names of many of the spirits, such as Azrael or Bael, correspond to those found in classical magical tradition. Others, however, have names that are not found in the area of magic, such as Rarum, Gibsir, Rahol, or Adica.

It is unclear where Bardon found these names. It is possible they stem from a medieval book of magic, or grimoire, such as *The Book of the Sacred Magic of Abramelin the Mage*. As its title suggests, the famed work of Abraham of Worms, which dates to 1458, is about the "true practice of age-old divine magic."

The magic mirror is not an indispensable article, however, it relieves the work of the magician and is a popular aid, especially for ritual magic and evocations. In some circumstances, it can replace the magical triangle.

AUSTIN OSMAN SPARE
FULFILLMENT OF SECRET DESIRES

A new system of magic

Austin Osman Spare (1886–1956), developer of the magic system of Zos Kia Cultus, is regarded as the founder of sigil magic. A sigil is a seal, from the Latin word *sigillum*, or "token, signet." A well-known seal is that of King Solomon, which illustrates the four elements along with their antitheses.

Spare was thoroughly familiar with psychiatric doctrines on the power of the unconscious as expounded by Freud. An artist by training, he was fascinated by the possibilities Freud's theories opened up for a new kind of magic system. As his interest in a career as an artist waned, he devoted more of his energy instead into developing a new form of magic. He published the results of his studies in *The Book of Pleasure (Self-Love). The Psychology of Ecstasy*.

Spare was considered an anarchist among magicians. For him, any ritual or technique and any faith were allowed, whether in God or Buddha.

Sigils and Zos Kia Cultus

Freud's psychology gave Spare the idea of anchoring the fulfillment of desires in the unconscious through magical rituals. This is done using a sigil, a symbolic, creative illustration of a certain wish that—together with a ritual—is firmly suggested, or anchored, to the unconscious while in a trance state and then consciously forgotten. This magical practice is said to be very effective.

The Zos Kia Cultus is a special form of occultism or magic. Zos is the sphere of the body, which is seen as a whole, and Kia is the divine self projected therein. According to Spare, magic is everywhere, and all techniques, forms of ritual and belief systems are permitted. As chaos magic will later put it, pray to God and also to Buddha; let the Devil help you together with the archangel. True belief does not comprise any beliefs. With his system, A. O. Spare brought creative anarchy to people's thinking about magic.

Austin Osman Spare was originally an artist. Aleister Crowley took notice of him at an exhibition including his pictures of grotesquely sexualized figures in the midst of numerous magical symbols—and Spare soon became a member of Crowley's AA order.

THE MAGIC
ORDER OF THE GOLDEN DAWN

No immortality without consecration

The practical work of the secret order of the Golden Dawn was based on the assumption that immortality can only be achieved when the earthly/human part of the human being allies itself with God. This information about the order comes from the magician Israel Regardie (1907–1985), who was a member of Golden Dawn, but broke his vow of secrecy in 1937. The order was founded in 1888 in London. In the beginning, the circle of magic enthusiasts limited their activities to intense study of magic books and conducting magical rituals. The order borrowed from the principles of the Kabbalah, the Rosicrucians, the Theosophists, and ancient Egyptian magic. There were ten different degrees within the structure of the order. The lowest degree was called "Zelator" and the ninth degree "Magus"—magician. The tenth degree, however, was "Ipsissimus:" a person who had found and was one with their true self. This placed them above the rank even of a magician.

Seven magic objects
Each person who was accepted into the order had to create seven magic objects: a goblet representing the element of water, a dagger for air, a disk for earth, a magic wand for fire, a sword for the fiery power of Mars, a lotus wand for conjuring, and a rose cross. Each of these insignia was associated with a specific color that formed a link between the spirit world and the material world. Color mysticism and Tarot cards formed the magical groundwork of this order. They were used to summon so-called astral visions, through which the initiates hoped to penetrate deep into the unconscious.

Initiation into the order, which was founded in 1888 under the name "Fraternity of the Esoteric Order of the Golden Dawn," required the new member to fabricate seven magical objects, including a goblet symbolizing the element of water.

The Jacob's ladder, which connects Heaven and Earth, plays an important role in the rituals of the Order of the Golden Dawn.

A kind of Jacob's ladder between Earth and Heaven

The ability to have prophetic dreams and to leave one's body via the soul are two of the primary goals of those who practice magic. The magician Aleister Crowley and Israel Regardie, mentioned above, did a great deal to publicize these magic practices as realized by the Golden Dawn. At the heart of these rituals was the idea of installing a kind of "Jacob's ladder" from Heaven to Earth in order to fully bring into play the four different bodies that were assumed to be within us—the mental, the emotional, the material and the astral—as a whole. Only then could magic be effective. The Order of the Golden Dawn broke up at the beginning of the twentieth century as a result of inner strife. The members of the Golden Dawn continued to practice magic and various other secret orders emerged from it, such as the Fraternity of Inner Light founded by Dion Fortune, which still exists today.

Bram Stoker, author of *Dracula*, was a member of the Order of the Golden Dawn. Stoker based the figure of Dracula on the fearsome Prince Vlad, who impaled (*dracul*) his victims.

Initiation into the order

The initiation ritual was by no means easy or pleasant for the candidates (called adepts). The psyches of the adepts were subject to systematic befuddlement until the Golden Dawn members felt they were ready for final initiation. "Loss of orientation in the dark" was how the order referred to this portion of the initiation ceremony, in which frightening experiences were suggested to the adepts, culminating in the "descent into Hell." The candidates may have been administered drugs beforehand in order to induce visions during the initiation ceremony that seemed like near-death experiences. They would imagine their soul leaving the body and ascending into other spheres in the realm of the beyond. At the end would come the "resurrection" or "rebirth"—if the person had withstood everything unscathed, which was not always the case.

The pentagram ritual practiced by the Golden Dawn

The pentagram ritual gives an idea of the kinds of ceremonies performed by this order. "Touch your forehead and say *ateh* (Thine is), the breast and say *malkuth* (the kingdom), the right shoulder and say *ve-geburah* (and the power), the left shoulder and say *ve-gebulah* (and the glory). Fold your hands and say *le-olam* (forever)." (6) This all took place by candlelight, which lent atmosphere to every magical undertaking. Inner composure and full concentration are required for the success of any ritual, along with strict observance of the prescribed sequence. Finally, the gods are invoked:

"Then draw a pentagram (five-pointed star) toward the East, point forcefully at its center and call the name JHVH (Yahweh), then draw a pentagram toward the South, call out *Adonai*, then a pentagram toward the West, call out *Eheie*, and then a pentagram toward the North, and call out *Agla* ..." (6)

Flaming pentagrams

Also invoked during pentagram rituals are the four archangels, while the practitioners imagine themselves surrounded by flaming pentagrams. Magic consists of

The pentagram was also an important element of the rituals of magic. In the Order of the Golden Dawn had the function of banishing Earth energies and was always drawn starting at the lower left.

precisely these kinds of rituals, which entail certain sequences of movement and the uttering of certain names. Breathing in the right rhythm is important as well, in order to summon the supernatural powers.

Aleister Crowley often claimed that the members of the Golden Dawn were not always friendly toward one another. As a result, battles were fought within the order, which took place on the astral plane. These demonstrated who among them ultimately had the most powerful magic at his or her command. Reading Dion Fortune's reports, it is easy to imagine that she was one adept who knew how to do battle on the astral plane.

The modern witches' movement gathered momentum in the mid-1900s, particularly in England.

WICCA
MODERN WITCHES AMONG US

Rebirth of witchcraft

The last witch on European soil was supposedly executed in Poznan, Poland in 1793. A good 100 years later, in 1899, a book was published by English writer and journalist Charles G. Leland (1824–1903) called *Aradia—The Gospel of the Witches*. Leland tells of meeting a young woman in Italy named Maddalena, who claimed to be the last descendant of a long line of witches. She not only revealed old rites and songs to Leland; she also claimed to be able to teach people witchcraft by assuming the persona of Aradia. *Aradia*—a new edition of which appeared in 1979—

became a classic adopted by the Wicca movement. Colin Lethbridge's 1962 book *Witches: Investigating an Ancient Religion* also had a profound influence on the emerging witches' covens.

Witches' covens

Witches' covens represent a modern revival of the old belief in witches. The word *coven* was used for the first time in 1662 during the interrogation of the Scottish witch Gowdie. Gowdie explained at the time that a coven was made up of thirteen witches. Others believe

One of the most prominent Wiccans is Miriam Santos, who calls herself Starhawk. She is an eco-feminist and peace activist who since 1979 has published several books on goddess religions. She also hosts frequent workshops all over the world.

that the thirtenth member of the coven is the Devil himself. Modern covens are interested not only in magic, but even more so in a feeling of belonging to the Earth goddess. *Wicca* literally means "witch," but connotes as well the ancient religion of the Great Goddess that was superseded by Christianity. Gerald B. Gardner, former director of the Witch Museum on the Isle of Man in England, tried to resurrect the long-lost lore of the "Old Religion" in 1954. His book *Witchcraft Today* laid the groundwork for the Wicca

cult. The first modern-day witches' covens were thus formed in England.

Starhawk—a modern witch

The most prominent contemporary American witch is Miriam Santos (born in 1951), who goes by the name of Starhawk. She has written a number of bestselling books and has been giving workshops on witchcraft since the 1970s, including some in Europe. Reading her books, one is reminded of Aleister Crowley and his maxim to "Do whatever you like!" God is a Goddess and everything that serves to promote one's individual development is allowed. However, Starhawk does qualify this by saying that witches are obligated to "honor and respect all living things." Only through human beings can the Goddess, who sustains all life, unfold her full beauty. For Starhawk, as the most well-known representative of American Wicca, magic is a way to unleash the hidden powers slumbering within us. Magic must be practiced every day by carrying out its rituals if it is to be effective. Starhawk claims that the magical practices, dances, and songs that she teaches are based on old traditions going back as far as the Stone Age, when women and men treated each other as equals.

Wicca in the USA

From the British Isles, the movement soon made its way over the ocean to the USA. In 1975, 13 naked "daughters of Wicca" gathered in the state of Washington for the first time. They celebrated their witches' sabbath once a month by candlelight, singing Latin psalms that were supposedly able to heal the sick and exorcise the souls of the dead. In 1977, the first known witches' wedding was celebrated: "The god of the witches is a god of love," recited the bridegroom, holding a sword in his hand. There are still practicing witches' covens in the USA today—according to a representative estimate in 2000, there are 10,000 in New York alone.

The Wiccans are not primarily interested in magic, but instead in their bond with the Earth goddess. They pray to the Great Goddess who was displaced long ago by male gods.

The old image of a witch as an ugly woman with warts on her nose and a cat on her shoulder is obsolete. Witches have become modern, keeping pace with the times. Today, they even offer their services over the Internet.

Nature and humans in balance

Above all, Starhawk and the Wicca movement are interested in recreating an equilibrium between humans and nature—not in order to do things one may associate with witchcraft (curses, Satanism, etc.), but instead as a means of returning to a primal female-centered religion. The Wicca cult worships the moon goddess Luna along with the ancient Greek goddesses Kybele and Diana. Each coven has a maximum of thirteen members who meet thirteen times a year, at the full moon. They celebrate their rituals at length,

dance, and invoke the great goddess. There are three degrees of initiation, which are kept secret, as are the formulas for their magic tinctures and salves. This much is known: every new candidate enters the circle of the other witches blindfolded. Either Diana, the goddess of the hunt, or Kybele is invoked. Kybele is the goddess of the underworld, in whose honor men in ancient times supposedly even castrated themselves while in an ecstatic trance. When the blindfold is finally removed, the new member greets the others in the coven with her new magic name.

Witches still cast spells

Anyone who thinks modern witches devote themselves exclusively to the practice of their pagan faith is quite mistaken. Some witches even offer their services on the Internet these days, and are prepared to cast evil spells for the right price. Curses are a form of magic that was already practiced by the Germanic tribes. Druids uttered curses when they wanted to injure or even kill someone. This works only if the affected person knows about it and willingly believes in the power that is trying to do him harm. In this sense, witches have always been able to cast effective spells. But for every spell there is also a counterspell. You need only ask the witch next door, provided you can find her.

The shaman Maria Sabina

The most important shaman of modern times, whose influence on the Wicca movement can hardly be overestimated, was Maria Sabina (1894–1985), a member of the Mazatec Indians from Mexico. She was known as the Wise Woman in her homeland, although she never went to school. In the 1960s, once she had given inquisitive ethnologists from the USA a look at the magic she worked, her fame spread far beyond the borders of her own country—as a healer and witch in the positive sense. Maria Sabina saw her life's work as surrendering herself to wisdom in order to use it to heal people from their illnesses. The powerful healer regarded herself as a daughter of the *Ninos Santos*, or "Holy Children," the term she used to refer to the native psilocybe mushrooms she used for her cures.

The holy mushrooms

Psilocybe mushrooms have been used by Mexico's Indians for several centuries. They produce visions and supposedly further the power to heal, as well. Scientific studies have shown that their hallucinogenic power is similar to that of LSD. Maria Sabina was allegedly able to heal many illnesses with the help of the mushrooms by going into a shamanic trance and undertaking journeys, like the shamans of Siberia, during which she appeased the spirits. Sabina said that she sometimes suffered greatly on these journeys to the otherworld. When she ingested mushrooms, it was always as part of a ceremony. An associate beat a drum in order to change the healer's state of consciousness. The drumbeat was to be synchronized with her heartbeat—one of the many forgotten techniques the Wicca movement has Sabina to thank for reviving. Many women in medieval Europe probably used healing methods similar to those practiced by Sabina, the difference being that their drug of choice was not a fungus, but instead the thorn apple (jimson weed).

The leaves and seeds of the thorn apple contain the poisonous alkaloid hyoscyamine. Witches used this substance, which triggers hallucinations, in their salves. The seeds are used in magic to incite fights.

Conclusion

Between magic and psi phenomena

Psi phenomena is a blanket term for paranormal manifestations such as telekinesis (the ability to move objects without physical contact) and telepathy (mind reading). To date, no conclusive evidence for the existence of such manifestations has been produced, but no counter-evidence is available, either, in the form of a purely rational explanation for known occurrences. In the case of hauntings by poltergeists, or knocking ghosts, the psychoses of those in whose immediate surroundings they occurred have often been found to trigger these phenomena, although this does not explain the seemingly supernatural events. Naturally, many mysterious apparitions have been exposed as trickery or the product of a lively imagination. Nevertheless, as is so often the case, many remain unexplained and enigmatic.

The claim is often made in relevant publications that it is possible to learn to move objects or read minds through magical exercises, but no magician has yet been able to offer any real proof.

Where does the journey end? The question of whether magical practices make it possible to move objects without touching them or to read minds remains unanswered. What is for certain is that many people let magic lure them onto unfamiliar terrain.

It may be that magic and parapsychology overlap somewhat, but the future will tell—namely, when studies and analysis of psi phenomena have advanced to the point that they can be reproduced in the laboratory. If this should ever become possible, magical practices might prove to offer a way of calling forth supernatural manifestations.

Rupert Sheldrake's sensational discovery

The theory propounded by English biochemist Rupert Sheldrake that there are so-called morphogenetic fields which, free of material and energy, nonetheless persist over time and space and form an invisible informative connection between living creatures could pave the way to new approaches in this field. Russian scientists such as Alexander Gurwitch are also working intensively on this theory, which could help explain phenomena such as telepathy, telekinesis, or ghostly apparitions. This kind of "field" is not limited to the brain, says Sheldrake, but extends beyond the body into surrounding space. All living things seem to be connected with each other through "resonance." This is also the approach taken by a new model for explaining magic: the conscious control of energy through information.

Right: Hauntings attributed to poltergeists or knocking ghosts have often been traced to severe psychic problems on the part of the haunted person. These problems can at least be seen as the catalyst for such mysterious phenomena, if not the cause.

Sources

1 Lamont-Brown, Raymond. *A Book of Witchcraft*. New York: Taplinger Publishing Co., 1971.

2 Regardie, Israel. *The Foundations of Practical Magic*. London: Aquarian Press, 1979.

3 Crowley, Aleister. *Magick in Theory and Practice*. Dover Publications, 1976.

4 Hasenfratz, Peter. *Die religiöse Welt der Germanen. Ritual, Magie, Kult, Mythos*. Freiburg: Herder, 1994.

5 Govinda, Anagarika. *The Inner Structure of the I'Ching*. New York: Weatherill Publishers, 1981.

6 Regardie, Israel. *The Golden Dawn, 6th edition*. St. Paul: Llewellyn, 2002.

7 Levi, Eliphas. *Magic: A History of its Rites, Rituals, and Mysteries*. Trans. Arthur Edward Waite. New York and London: Dover Publications, 2006.

8 Fortune, Dion. *Psychic Self-Defense, rev. ed.* York Beach: Samuel Weiser Inc., 2001.

9 Bardon, Franz. *Der Weg zum wahren Adepten*. Wuppertal: Rüggeberg, 2002.

Ashley, Leonard R. N. *Geschichte der Magie*. Bergisch-Gladbach: Komet, 2000.

Bardon, Franz. *The Practice of Magical Evocation: Instructions for Invoking Spirits from the Spheres Surrounding Us*. Trans. Peter Dimai. NM: Brotherhood of Life, 1984.

Biedermann, Hans. *Handlexikon der Magischen Künste*. Munich: Droemer Knaur, 1976.

Braem, Harald. *Magische Riten und Kulte*. Munich, 1995.

Daxelmüller, Christoph. *Zauberpraktiken*. Düsseldorf: Albatros Verlag, 2001.

Dee, John. *Monas Hieroglyphica*. Whitefish: Kessinger Publishing, 2003.

Dehn, Georg, Ed. Abraham of Worms. *Book of Abramelin*. Melbourne: Ibis Publishing, 2006.

Donner-Grau, Florinda. *The Witch's Dream: A Healer's Way of Knowledge*. New York: Penguin, 1997.

Ebeling, Florian. *Das Geheimnis des Hermes Trismegistos. Geschichte des Hermetismus*. Munich, 2005.

Endres, Franz Carl / Schimmel, Annemarie. *Das Mysterium der Zahl*. Munich, 1996.

Fortune, Dion. *Cosmic Doctrine*. York Beach: Samuel Weiser, 2000.

Fortune, Dion. *Mystical Qabalah, rev. ed.* York Beach: Samuel Weiser, 2000.

Gardner, Gerald B. *Witchcraft Today*. Sacramento: Citadel Press, 2004.

Golowin, Sergius. *Die Magie der verbotenen Märchen. Von Hexendrogen und Feenkräuterrn*. Hamburg: Merlin Verlag, 1978.

Graves, Robert. *The White Goddess*. London: Allen Lane, 2000.

Gregorius, Gregor A., ed. *Aleister Crowley's magische Rituale*. Berlin, 1980.

Holroyd, Stuart. *The Elements of Gnosticism*. Element Books, 1997.

Hornung, Eric. *Das geheime Wissen der Ägypter*. Munich: DTV, 2003.

Leland, Charles G., ed. *Aradia: Gospel of the Witches*. Seattle: Phoenix Publishing, 2000.

Levi, Eliphas. *Transcendental Magic*. York Beach: Weiser Books, 2001.

Lucadou, Walter. *Dimension PSI – Fakten zur Parapsychologie*. Berlin: List, 2003.

Picture credits

Corbis: 2 Clayton J. Price, 4 Gianni Dagli Orti, 5 Brooklyn Museum of Art (l.), Hulton-Deutsch Collection (r.), 6 Bettmann, 7 Stapleton Collection, 8 Stapleton Collection, 9 Stefano Bianchetti (a.), Corbis (b.), 11 Gianni Dagli Orti, 12 Roger Wood, 13 The Art Archive, 14 Roger Wood, 15 Michael Nicholson, 16 Bettmann, 17 Gianni Dagli Orti (a.), STScI/NASA (b.), 19 Brooklyn Museum of Art, 20 Blasius Erlinger/zefa, 22 Bettmann, 23 PoodlesRock (a.), The Cover Story (b.), 24 Richard T. Nowitz, 25 Jacqui Hurst (l.), Sandro Vannini (r.), 26 Alen MacWeeney, 27 Archivo Iconografico, S.A. (a.), Gianni Dagli Orti (b.), 28 Hans Georg Roth (a.), Caroline Penn (b.), 29 Christine Osborne, 30 SETBOUN, 31 Stefano Bianchetti (a.), Dave Bartruff (b.), 32 Gianni Dagli Orti (a.), Courtesy of Museum of St. Pere de Galligants; Ramon Manent (b.), 33 SETBOUN, 34 Burstein Collection, 35 Robert Estall (a.), Ted Spiegel (c.), 36 Jose Fuste Raga, 37 Yang Liu, 38 Stuart Westmorland, 39 Tim Page, 40 Les Stone/Sygma, 41 Archivo Iconografico, S.A. (a.), Stefano Bianchetti (b.), 42 Bob Krist (a.), Michael Freeman (b.), 43 Les Stone/Sygma, 44 Jennifer Kennard, 45 Bettmann, 46 Rainer Holz/zefa, 47 Bettmann (a.), Jose Fuste Raga (b.), 48 Geray Sweeney, 49 Sergio Pitamitz/zefa, 50 Historical Picture Archive, 51 Bettmann (a.), Werner Forman (b.), 52 Bettmann, 53 Werner Forman, 54 Lindsay Hebberd, 55 Bowers Museum of Cultural Art (a.), Corbis (b.), 56 Chris Rainier, 57 David Turnley, 58 Bob Krist, 59 Randy Faris, 60 Bettmann, 61 Reuters (a.), Roger Wood (b.), 62 Hulton-Deutsch Collection, 63 The Cover Story, 65 Hulton-Deutsch Collection, 66 Bettmann, 67 Hulton-Deutsch Collection, 68 Hulton-Deutsch Collection, 69 Bettmann, 71 Ruggero Vanni (a.), Stuart Westmorland (b.), 72 Pallava Bagla (a.), Stapleton Collection (b.), 74 Mark Hamilton/zefa, 75 Historical Picture Archive, 76 Bettmann (b.), 77 Historical Picture Archive, 78 Massimo Listri, 79 Craig Tuttle, 81 W. Cody, 82 Gary Salter/zefa, 83 B.M.W./zefa, 84 Alen MacWeeney (a.), Hulton-Deutsch Collection (b.), 85 David Lees, 86 Gerrit Greve (a.), Hulton-Deutsch Collection (b.), 87 The Cover Story, 88 The Cover Story, 89 Archivo Iconografico, S.A. (b.), 90 Cynthia Hart Designer, 91 Stapleton Collection, 92 Al Francekevich, 93 Bettmann

Parapirctures Archiv: 21, 80

Stempell, Kyra: 70, 73, 76 (a.), 89 (a.)

Regardie, Israel: *Die Elemente der Magie*. Hamburg, 1991.

Roberts, Marc. *Das neue Lexikon der Esoterik*. Munich, 1995.

Schubart, Walter. *Religion und Eros*. Munich: C.H. Beck, 1966.

Seligmann, Kurt. *The History of Magic*. New York: Pantheon Books, 1948.

Sheldrake, Rupert. *Das schöpferische Universum*. Berlin: Ullstein, 1993.

Spare, Austin O. *Das Buch der ekstatischen Freude*. Holdenstedt, 1996.

INDEX